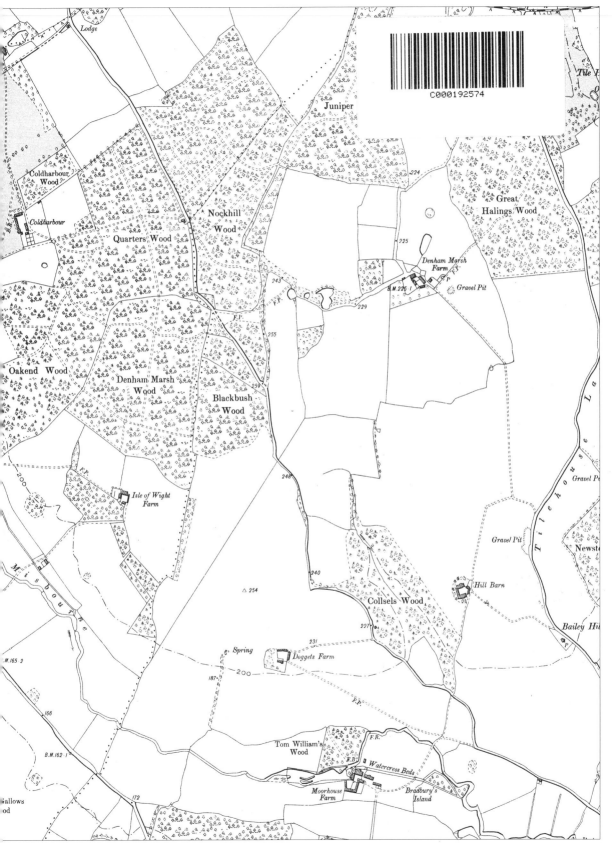

Lodge

Coldharbour
Wood

Coldharbour

Juniper

Nockhill
Wood

Quarters Wood

224

Great
Halings Wood

225

Denham Marsh
Farm

B.M.225

Gravel Pit

243

229

F.P.

F.P.

255

Oakend Wood

Denham Marsh
Wood

Blackbush
Wood

259

248

Isle of Wight
Farm

F.P.

200

Gravel Pit

Gravel Pit

Newst

△ 254

240

Hill Barn

Collsels Wood

Bailey Hi

227

Misbourne

Spring

231

Doggets Farm

187

200

M.165 2

166

F.P.

Tom William's
Wood

F.B.

B.M.162

F.B.

F.B.

Watercress Beds

Moorhouse
Farm

Bradbury's
Island

allows
od

172

Tilehouse La

Ordnance Survey 6in: 1 mile, 1900

GERRARDS CROSS
A History

An architect's impression of new shops at Gerrards Cross, 1907, signed by Walter F.C. Holden, then an assistant to the architects, Kerkham, Burgess & Myers.

GERRARDS CROSS
A History

Julian Hunt
and
David Thorpe

Phillimore

2006

Published by
PHILLIMORE & CO. LTD
Shopwyke Manor Barn, Chichester, West Sussex, England

© Julian Hunt and David Thorpe, 2006

ISBN 1 86077 388 5

Printed and bound in Great Britain by
CAMBRIDGE PRINTING

Contents

List of Illustrations

Frontispiece: Station Parade, 1907

Acknowledgements

❖

The authors owe a special debt of gratitude to Harvey Parr, who has project managed this book and the accompanying exhibition to be staged at Gerrards Cross in April 2006. They would also like to pay tribute to Barbara Lyddiatt and Charlotte Morrison, who spent many days working in the Centre for Buckinghamshire Studies in Aylesbury, helping to list the collection of Eton Rural District Council building regulations plans. The style and content of this book is heavily influenced by the house plans made by the various architects working in Gerrards Cross between 1906 and 1939. Permission to use these drawings has been given by South Bucks District Council and by A. & Q. Partners of Beaconsfield.

The majority of the photographic illustrations have come from the collection of Colin Seabright of Chesham Bois, nos. 2-3, 10-1, 13, 15-6, 21, 24, 26-31, 34, 39-40, 42, 47, 49, 51, 62-4, 72, 77, 79-80, 86-7, 99, 109, 135, 149 and 154. Official sources of illustrations include Beaconsfield Historical Society, nos. 41 and 71; Birmingham Reference Library, no. 12; Centre for Buckinghamshire Studies, nos. 4, 17, 19, 22-3, 25, 32, 36-8, 44-6, 48, 54-6, 59, 61, 65, 81, 88, 89, 101, 104, 126, 134, 140, 146-8; Cornwall Record Office, no. 20; Gerrards Cross and Chalfont St Peter Historical Society, no.78; Royal Institute of British Architects Library, nos. 67, 91, 123 and 131; and Worcestershire Record Office, no. 57. Other illustrations are from Abbeyfield Gerrards Cross Society, no. 90; Audrey Baker, no. 7; Buckinghamshire Advertiser, no. 14; Hamptons International, no. 70; Keith Hyllier, no. 102; David Lovell, nos. 95, 105, 108 and 145; and Colin Smythe, nos. 6, 8-9, 35, 50, 60, and 97. Information and assistance has been provided by the Archivist, Brasenose College, Oxford, Michael Brogden of WEC International, Ian Colston, John Dodd, Doug Freeman, Alan, John and Nicola Frost, Raymond Glenny, Gerry Hoare, Ian Johnson of B.P. Collins & Co., Trevor Kent, Anthony Lock of Thorpe House School, David Lovell, Peter Lomas, Robin Morrison, Peter Roberts, Geoffrey Seagrove, Nigel Stewart-Wallace, Kareen Stuart, Bill Taylor, A.P. Whitley and James Worthington.

Special thanks are due to Buckinghamshire County Council, Gerrards Cross Parish Council and South Bucks District Council for their support in producing this book and to The Frost Partnership, Hamptons International and the Roberts Newby Partnership, sponsors of the accompanying exhibition.

Foreword

The project to celebrate the centenary of the coming of the railway to Gerrards Cross started in October 2003 when the Bucks Archaeological Society held its Annual History Conference at the Memorial Centre, Gerrards Cross. The highlight of the day was a guided tour of Gerrards Cross led by David Thorpe. At the Gerrards Cross Summer School in August 2004, a day school on the history of Gerrards Cross was given by Julian Hunt. From this emerged an exhibition planning group, including Trevor Kent, Barbara Lyddiatt, Charlotte Morrison and Councillor Jennifer Woolveridge, soon to be joined by Harvey Parr, Councillor Malcolm Barres-Baker and Nigel Halliday.

The group were keenly aware of the planning crisis facing Gerrards Cross and many similar towns and villages, where soaring land values are causing developers to demolish the very houses which make these settlements so attractive. Even during the preparation of this book several fine houses have been lost, to be replaced by flats or houses of little architectural merit. It is the hope of our team that by drawing attention to the best architecture in Gerrards Cross we can save key buildings from this destructive process. We are fortunate indeed that some of the finest British architects of the early 20th century left their mark on Gerrards Cross. We have buildings by nationally known architects such as Baillie Scott, P. Morley Horder, Forbes & Tate and Edgar Ranger, and by excellent local architects such as Burgess, Holden & Watson and Robert G. Muir. Gerrards Cross was indeed the home of Y.J. Lovell and Son, whose houses featured year after year at the Ideal Home Exhibition. It is our duty to preserve their work, and, where redevelopment does take place, to encourage developers to commission architects and builders of equal imagination and skill. To do otherwise may eventually produce a settlement so devoid of charm as to lower, rather than raise, property values.

I would like to thank Julian Hunt and David Thorpe for bringing our group together and for enabling us to produce this permanent record of our unique community.

JENNIFER WOOLVERIDGE
GERRARDS CROSS PARISH COUNCIL, 2006

Introduction

This book commences with the histories of several great houses which, although situated in five different parishes, all came to give their address as Gerrards Cross. It was the concentration of such genteel households around Gerrards Cross Common which gradually gave character to the area and caused it to be called 'The Brighton of Bucks', at least forty years before the district was opened up by the railway. The book goes on to analyse the occupations and social position of the original residents and compares them with the origins and aspirations of the newcomers who settled here after the opening of the railway in 1906. The book then describes the process of building the new houses, highlighting the architects, builders and estate agents who shaped the modern Gerrards Cross. The authors hope to show that Gerrards Cross, far from lacking history, has ancient and fascinating origins and an architectural heritage which makes it one of the most desirable places in this country in which to live.

This account of the history of Gerrards Cross is selective. We have limited overlap with earlier studies such as those by Edmonds and Baker. After exploring some earlier topics, the focus is on the 19th and the first 40 years of the 20th centuries, the period when Gerrards Cross became a parish and then a special type of suburban village. In this it draws on sources that were either not available to the earlier authors, or were not fully utilised by them. The data that has emerged from them is very rich. It not only forms the basis for much of this book but is also to be used in a companion volume, *An Historical Atlas of Gerrards Cross 1840-1940*, and may be presented in other forms.

In one respect there is a gap in the source material. This is the detail of the 1911 Census that will become available only in 2011 or shortly after. Since this will tell us much more about the first residents of the railway suburb, it is intended to extend the current account then. In this respect, as a study in progress, the authors would welcome material to fill out the account. In particular, they want to learn more about the motives that brought the first new residents, and the retailers who served them, to Gerrards Cross. Such material may lie hidden in private hands and in the work of family historians.

For the purposes of this study, Gerrards Cross has been defined as an area larger than that of the modern parish. It includes that part of Chalfont St Peter approximately south of School Lane, including Austenwood Common, which for much of the 20th century carried a Gerrards Cross postal address.

One

Gerrards Cross in its Geographical Setting

❖

The fact that Gerrards Cross is not mentioned in Domesday Book does not mean that the area was not settled at the time, or that it lacked significance. The British hill fort now surrounded by Camp Road is one of the largest fortifications in Buckinghamshire and was clearly a centre where the population of a wide area could seek protection in times of trouble. By 1086, any British tribal boundaries had long since been replaced by those of Roman and then Saxon estates, but it appears that a topographical feature like Bulstrode Camp, and the large area of open land which surrounded it, did not fit easily into the parish system. The new parishes north of the Thames were arranged in long thin strips so that each had meadows and arable near the river and summer pastures and woodland to the north. The tax assessments made in 1086 on the manors of Chalfont St Peter, Iver, Langley Marish and Upton cum Chalvey must have taken into account their respective claims to the area of waste land first known as Chalfont Heath, and later as Gerrards Cross Common.

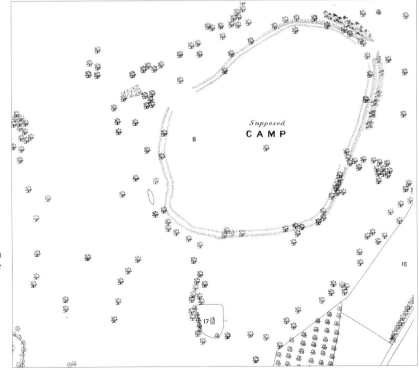

1 Bulstrode Camp, from the 1st Edition Ordnance Survey Map, 1876.

1

These parishes shared the rich resources of the Heath, including summer pasture, water from the ponds, wood for building and fuel, and clay for bricks, tiles and pots. At some early period, their conflicting claims must have been resolved by marking out boundaries defining the area of the Heath belonging to each parish.

The largest portion of Chalfont Heath was naturally within the parish of Chalfont St Peter, and extended north-east from the Oxford Road, up to the area of common arable land called Latchmoor Field. The eastern part, straddling the Oxford Road, belonged to the parish of Iver, where the estates called Oak End and Woodhill were established at an early date. The northern part of Langley Marish also had a boundary on Chalfont Heath. Here was land called Alderbourne, belonging to Ankerwyke Priory, Wraysbury, and a farmstead called Prestwicks, meaning the priest's farm. Fulmer does not appear in Domesday Book but it soon afterwards emerged as a separate parish, including the ancient hill fort and that portion of Chalfont Heath south-west of the Oxford Road which the locals called Fulmer Heath, or Fulmer Common. A further part of Chalfont Heath, west of the hill fort, belonged to Upton cum Chalvey. This extended over 123 acres and became the site for the mansion called Bulstrode Park. The boundary between Fulmer and this detached portion of Upton cum Chalvey was an old road, marked on the 1686 Bulstrode Estate map, which was a continuation of Bull Lane, crossing the Oxford Road near to the *Bull Inn*.[1]

Early References to Gerrards Cross

The editor of a 1921 directory addressed the issue of the lack of history in Gerrards Cross by relating the local tradition of the origin of the name. He told his readers that in the days of the stage coach, 'Gerrard' or 'Jarrett' had been a popular landlord of a coaching inn, situated where the road to Slough crossed the Oxford Road. He suggested that the publican's name had clung to the spot long after the inn had been demolished. This plausible story is repeated in many guide books to Buckinghamshire and the Chilterns, but in reality Gerrards Cross is much older than the stage coach.

There are, however, many earlier references to the place-name 'Gerrards Cross'. As early as 1448, a rental of the Abbot of Missenden's manor at Chalfont St Peter lists a William Bulstrode paying 12d. per year for 'land in the field near Geraddescrosse'. In a Chalfont St Peter court roll of 1555, a tenant is fined 12d. for cutting down two trees at 'Gerarde Crosse on le hethe'.[2] More dramatically, the Chalfont St Peter parish register in November 1580 records the burial of 'Thomas Davyes murthered by one Richard Hassell at Jarretts Crosse'.

These references establish the antiquity of Gerrards Cross, but they do not tell us which 'Gerrard' was so fondly remembered, or so deeply feared, that his name was attached to the place. One candidate appears in a survey of Chalfont St Peter, probably prepared for the Abbot of Missenden, about 1333. It lists Nicholas le Plomer the elder and Nicholas le Plomer the younger as holding a quarter of a virgate of land of 'Gerard of Chalfont'.[3] It is not clear where this land was, but the document does show that 'Gerrard' was a Christian name used by at least one wealthy family in Chalfont St Peter in the 14th century.

The editor of the 1921 directory took the 'cross' in Gerrards Cross to refer to the cross-roads in the centre of the Common, where the road to Slough crosses the Oxford Road. All the early travellers maps and estate maps, however, locate Gerrards or 'Jarretts' Cross at the west end of Chalfont Heath, near to Latchmoor Pond and to the *Bull Inn*. If the name does refer to a crossroads, it may have been at that point where Bull Lane once crossed the Oxford Road and continued down to Hedgerley Lane.

It was probably this road which was diverted by the Earl of Portland, with the consent of his neighbours, in 1707.

Most English place-names including the 'cross' element, however, refer to a boundary cross, or the mark of an important meeting place. A likely place for such a cross would be the point on the Oxford Road where the western side of Chalfont Heath was divided between Chalfont St Peter and Fulmer. The cross referred to in the place-name may even have been one of a series of crosses marking another boundary. It was common for religious houses to mark the boundary of their remote properties with a circuit of crosses. Temple Bulstrode, an estate within Hedgerley, which bounded the Oxford Road and had belonged successively to the Knights Templar, the Knights Hospitaller, Burnham Abbey and, from 1337 until the Dissolution of the Monasteries, to Bisham Abbey, may have been defined in this way.

Latchmoor Pond

Whether the name Gerrards Cross referred to a crossroads, a waymark or an estate boundary, it must have been a welcome stopping place on the great road from London to Oxford. The nearby Latchmoor Pond would have been a rare but vital source of drinking water for travellers and their pack-horses as they crossed the high ground between Uxbridge and Beaconsfield. The pond would have been especially useful to those driving animals to London, or to more local markets. The place-name Latchmoor is something of a tautology, being made up of *lache*, Middle English for a bog, and *mere*, Old English for a pool. Latchmoor Pond must indeed be ancient, for it gave its name to the common arable field called Latchmoor Field on which much of modern Gerrards Cross was built. It was only natural that farmers in the vicinity of the pond should have sold beer to the better-off travellers and drovers

passing along the Oxford Road and that the more popular beerhouses became inns like the *Bull Inn*.

The Oxford Road

As early as the 16th century, the poor condition of English roads was seen as a great obstacle to economic development. Roads were barely adequate to get produce to local markets and the surfaces were so poor that most goods were carried by pack-horses rather than wagons. In order to promote internal commerce, an Act of 1555 made every parish responsible for the repair of its own roads. Churchwardens appointed surveyors who were to encourage every parishioner to spend up to four days a year working on the roads. In 1563, a further Act increased the number of days to six and made Justices of the Peace responsible for ensuring that parishes fulfilled their obligations. These Acts would place a particular burden on parishes like Chalfont St Peter and Fulmer, whose boundary was the great road from London to Oxford. In 1573, the tenants of the manor of Temple Bulstrode agreed to repair the part of the king's highway leading from Beaconsfield to 'Gerardescrosse' that lay in the parish of Hedgerley.[4] The next year, Edward Bulstrode was ordered to repair the king's highway leading from 'Steppy lane towards Gerardes Crosse'. Henry Bulstrode of Bulstrode Park evidently took advantage of the system, as he is accused in the Chalfont St Peter court rolls in 1606 of having encroached on the waste, 'being the king's highway leading from Gerardes Crosse towards Beaconsfield, with a great ditch and hedge'.[5]

Turnpike Acts

English trade increased dramatically during the 17th century, making the inadequacies of the road network even more obvious. Tacitly admitting that forced labour was insufficient to repair the nation's roads, Parliament passed an

Act in 1662 enabling parish surveyors to levy a highways rate to be spent on road maintenance. The first successful attempt to relieve parishes of the duty to maintain a major road, and make the carriers and ordinary travellers pay instead, came in 1663. In that year, a private Act of Parliament was passed, enabling the Justices of the Peace of Hertfordshire to charge tolls and apply the proceeds to repairing a 15-mile section of the Great North Road near Royston. The success of this scheme led to the formation of other trusts, where local Justices of the Peace managed sections of major roads where they passed through particularly difficult terrains. The 1706 Act, which authorised the charging of tolls on a 15-mile stretch of Watling Street from Fornhill in Bedfordshire to Stony Stratford in Buckinghamshire, established an even greater precedent. The Act gave the power to charge tolls, not to the Justices of the Peace, but to a committee of local gentry and tradesmen. This set the pattern for the formation of local trusts to maintain main roads across the country for the next 150 years. The toll roads became known as 'turnpikes', as the gates erected across the roads where tolls were to be collected resembled the spiked barriers, or 'turnpikes', more familiar at castle gates.

The first part of the road from London to Oxford to be turnpiked was the 15-mile section from Tyburn to Uxbridge, for which an Act of Parliament was passed in 1715. Two Acts passed in 1719 turnpiked the 12-mile section from Beaconsfield to Stokenchurch and a further 18 miles from Stokenchurch to Oxford. Maintenance of the eight miles of the Oxford Road from Uxbridge to Beaconsfield remained the responsibility of the parish surveyors for another 30 years. The missing link in the local turnpike network was put in place by an Act of 1751, which turnpiked 'the road leading from the west end of the said town of Wendover to the end of a lane called Oak Lane, next to the great road called the Oxford Road,

lying between the town of Beaconsfield in the said County of Bucks, and Uxbridge in the County of Middlesex, and that part of the said great road which leads from the west end of the said town of Beaconsfield to the River Colne near Uxbridge.' The Act claimed that these roads were 'very deep and founderous, and inconvenient and dangerous to persons and carriages passing the same'. It gave responsibility for maintaining these two sections of road to the Buckingham to Wendover Turnpike Trust, which had been in operation since 1720. To the list of existing trustees were added over 80 gentlemen from the south of the county, including Lord George Bentinck, brother of the owner of Bulstrode Park, the Rev. Winch Holdsworth, Vicar of Chalfont St Peter, Lister Selman, owner of Chalfont Park, and Richard Whitchurch, lord of the manor of Chalfont St Peter.

In the 1770s, responsibility for maintaining the roads from Wendover to Oak Lane and Beaconsfield to Uxbridge passed to separate turnpike trusts. An Act of 1777 created a new trust to repair the road from the west end of the town of Wendover to the end of a lane called Oak Lane, next the great road called the Oxford Road, and also half a mile of road from the River Colne towards Beaconsfield. Another trust was established by an Act of 1779 to repair the Oxford Road from the west end of the town of Beaconsfield to within half a mile of the River Colne, near Uxbridge. Curiously, the remaining half mile of road into Uxbridge was repaired by the Wendover to Oak Lane End Trust as late as 1852.

Toll Collectors' Houses

Travellers on the Wendover to Oak Lane End road had to pass toll collectors' houses at the west end of Great Missenden and at the bottom of Gravel Hill, Chalfont St Peter. A new toll collector's house was built at Great Missenden in 1827 and that at Chalfont St

Peter was replaced with a new turnpike house at Oak End in 1828. Travellers on the Oxford Road passed toll gates opposite the *Dog and Duck*, Denham, at Red Hill, near the turn to Amersham, at Holtspur, west of Beaconsfield, and at London Road, High Wycombe. All of these toll houses have been demolished, but the ornate toll house at High Wycombe was moved in 1978 and rebuilt at the Chiltern Open Air Museum. Several of the milestones erected by the turnpike trustees survive, notably those at either end of Gerrards Cross Common.

The early turnpike Acts gave trustees powers to charge tolls and to repair the roads for a period of 21 years only. There were four acts for the Wendover to Oak Lane End Road: 1751, 1777, 1812 and 1833. The last Act, however, extended the trustees' powers for 31 years plus the period to the end of the parliamentary session then in progress. Similarly, there were five Acts for the Beaconsfield to Uxbridge Road: 1751, 1779, 1806, 1828 and 1852. The last Act of 1852 was known as the Beaconsfield and Red Hill Road Act and moved responsibility for repairing the last half mile of road into Uxbridge from the Trustees of the Wendover to Oak Lane End Road to those of the Beaconsfield and Red Hill Road. The powers conferred on the trustees by this Act were to continue in force for only 12 years plus the time remaining in the parliamentary session then in progress. This meant that the powers of the Wendover to Oak Lane Trustees and those of the Beaconsfield and Red Hill Trustees would expire in the same year.

With the opening of the London to Birmingham Railway, and part of the London to Bristol Railway in 1838, income from tolls on coaches and carriers' carts declined rapidly. The Wendover to Oak Lane trustees' powers expired in 1865 and the trust was wound up in the following year. The toll collector's house at Oak End was sold to John Nembhard Hibbert, of Chalfont Park, for £65. The funds still in the treasurer's hands were divided between the parishes which would once again be liable to repair their sections of the road. Chalfont St Peter received £10 17s. 0d.[6] The trustees of the Beaconsfield and Red Hill Turnpike closed their accounts in 1867. The toll houses at Denham and at Red Hill were sold in December 1867 to Benjamin Way of Denham Place for £25 each.[7] The Red Hill toll house was demolished for road widening in January 1929 and the Denham toll house was taken down in February 1931.[8]

Coaching Inns

The inns on the Oxford Road at Gerrards Cross pre-date the turnpike era, having provided accommodation both for travellers and their horses from at least the mid-17th century. Each inn would have an ostler on hand to replace the stage coach horses, whilst the passengers took refreshment during the 15 or so minutes allowed for the stop. The innkeepers would also hire out horses to pull private coaches to similar inns in the next large town.

Beaconsfield and High Wycombe, being respectable towns roughly half-way between London and Oxford, had several inns catering for those who wanted to break their journey overnight. One such inn was owned by Edward Marshall of High Wycombe, who died in 1698. The inventory attached to his will lists all the furniture, fire irons, bedding, carpets, curtains and tapestries in 16 guest rooms. Each room was named after an important visitor, such as the King's Chamber, the Queen's Chamber, or the Duke's Room, or given the name of a coach which changed horses at the inn, including the *Fleur de Lis*, the *Phoenix* or the *Worcester*. The prizers also listed goods in Mr Marshall's own room and those of his ostler and maids. Debts owing to the deceased included £8 from Mr Edward Bartlett of Oxford, coach master, and two sums of £20 and £40 owed by 'Mr Moore that keeps the Oxford stage coach'.[9]

2   The *Bull Inn*, Gerrards Cross, 1910.

In 1836, the following coaches passed through Gerrards Cross on their way to London: the *Union*, from Birmingham; the *Berkeley Hunt*, from Cheltenham; the *Regulator* and the *Retaliator*, both from Gloucester; the *Champion*, from Hereford; the *Blenheim* and the *Age*, from Oxford; The Thame Safety Coach and J. Coles Omnibus, both from Thame; the *Hope*, from Warwick; and the *Sovereign*, the *Telegraph*, the *Paul Pry* and the *Royal Mail*, all from Worcester.[10]

Lady Charlotte Blount, daughter of the Duke of Somerset, told her son, Oscar Blount, what seems a rather tall story, of the coaches passing the gates of Bulstrode Park at this time. 'It was the usual thing on a fine morning to walk up to the lodge gates at Gerrards Cross to see the mail coaches go up and down the great Oxford Road. Outside the park gates was an old elm tree and seven feet or so from the ground it was studded over with large nails and here the post boys used to fasten up their tired horses and leave them to cool. Lord Algernon St Maur, Lady Charlotte's youngest brother, was very fond of driving the mail coaches. He used to drive the stage from Wycombe to Gerrards Cross very often. One afternoon, coming down Du Pre's pitch at Wilton Park, the off-side wheeler kicked over the traces. The passengers begged him to pull up and put things straight. Not at all, said his lordship, the mail is late and I can only reach the *Bull Hotel*, Gerrards Cross by not stopping. I hope to be on time. He was punctual to the minute. Being in the

Blues he often drove the mail on the Bath Road from the Barracks at Windsor.'[11]

The *Bull Inn*

The *Oxford Arms* at Gerrards Cross, later called the *Bull Inn*, was not in the same league as Edward Marshall's inn in Wycombe. It did, however, feature on the Bulstrode Estate map of 1686, where it is represented as having three gables fronting the road. In 1689, the *Oxford Arms* was leased by the then owner of Bulstrode, Lady Jeffreys, to Robert Tibby, innholder, for 21 years.[12] On such a desolate stretch of road as that crossing Gerrards Cross Common, the *Oxford Arms* would be a very welcome site, especially to a cold and hungry traveller from London who had been shaken about in a primitive stage coach for the best part of a day. With poor road surfaces, there was a very real risk of the coach being overturned, especially in the winter. The fear of being held up by highwaymen was also real. The Buckinghamshire Quarter Sessions Records of 1692 includes the petition of Joseph Perkyns, ostler at the *Oxford Arms* at Gerrards Cross in Fulmer, stating that 'in December last, going with arms to defend a wagon loaded with their Majesty's money that was assaulted by several thieves and robbed near the said inn, the said thieves discharged two pistols upon him'.[13]

With the partial turnpiking of the Oxford Road in 1719, some increase in traffic was to be expected. By 1735, the Duke of Portland's agent, Bartholomew Druly, was prepared to repair and enlarge the inn. He drew up an agreement with John Dibley of Gerrards Cross, innholder, whereby the inn, now known as the *Bull Inn*, was leased for 21 years at £30 per year, plus £5 per year for every £100 the Duke was to expend on repairs. The building was to be extended on both sides. At the north-west corner of the house, an arched vault was to be built, supporting a pantry and scullery above, with a garret in the roof. Between the east end of the house and the packhorse stable, a parlour

was to be built, with a lodging room over it and a garret in the roof. These rooms were to be heated with a new chimney and the whole was to be of such a size as not to exclude light from the windows of the present house. The present scullery was to be converted into a room for guests and the stairs which went up to the room were to be moved. Sash windows were to be put in the new building next to the road, and the windows, doors, cornice and balcony were to be repainted.[14] Despite these improvements, the *Bull Inn* was not a coaching inn in the full sense of the word, as most of the Oxford and Worcester coaches changed horses at Uxbridge and then at Beaconsfield. It catered rather for travellers in private coaches who might choose to avoid the busier inns, and for visitors to Bulstrode Park and other genteel houses in the vicinity. The *Bull Inn* was also well-known to members of the Old Berkeley Hunt, who had kennels at Gerrards Cross at least as early as 1792.

The innkeepers at the *Bull* during the 18th century were William Wilson, 1746-80; his widow Mary, 1781-3; Philip Milton, 1784; Thomas Scott, 1785-95; and Thomas Hunt, 1796-1802.[15] When the able-bodied men of the county were listed in 1798 (the Posse Comitatus), Thomas Hunt of Fulmer is listed as a victualler, but the compiler notes that he is infirm. Two ostlers are also listed, John Lambourn and Daniel Stevens, suggesting that the inn was involved in the coaching trade at the time. Thomas Hunt's widow, Elizabeth, was the licensee from 1803-15. The *Bull Inn* was included in the sale of the Bulstrode Estate in 1810, when it was leased to Elizabeth Hunt, widow, at an annual rent of only £32 10s. It was described in the sale catalogue as a 'messuage and lands situate in the Parishes of Fulmer and Chalfont St Peter, consisting of … a brick messuage called the *Bull Inn*, at Gerrards Cross, on the high road from London to Oxford, with ample stabling, outbuildings, yards and garden'.[16]

The *Bull Inn* was subsequently sold to Weller's Amersham Brewery. Later innkeepers included William Hawkes, 1816-21; William Hawkes the younger, 1822-6; John Sanderson, 1827; Thomas Raveny, 1847-54; Anthony Girardet, 1864; Lewis Cook, 1869; Robert Bollan, 1872; Thomas Samworth, 1877-83; Thomas Lancaster, 1887; Samuel Anstey, 1891-5; George Ratcliff, 1899; Fredrick Brooker, 1903; and James Brooker, 1907-15.

The days of coaching were numbered from 1838, when the first section of Brunel's Great Western Railway was opened. Travellers to Gerrards Cross could alight at Slough and take a coach for the remaining eight miles. In 1851, Thomas Raveney at the *Bull Inn* still employed a post boy to ride with the coach horses and bring them back from the next stage. By 1856, however, the G.W.R. had opened their branch to Uxbridge, where a horse bus from the *Bull Inn*, Gerrards Cross, met the trains. The *Bull Inn* must have become difficult to manage for there were 11 different publicans from 1847 to 1907. In 1918, the freehold of the *Bull Inn* was bought by Sir John Ramsden, who used it as accommodation for staff working at Bulstrode Park. After the Bulstrode sale in 1932, the *Bull Inn* passed to Rock Development Ltd, who re-opened the *Bull Inn* to the public. They added a two-storey wing on the east side in 1932 and a ballroom on the west side in 1935. Further extensions were made under the style of Messrs Ethorpe Ltd. As Gerrards Cross became more and more fashionable in the 20th century, the *Bull Hotel* continued to expand along the Oxford Road and to the rear, facing Bulstrode Park. The *Bull Hotel* is now owned by Sarova Hotels and has 123 bedrooms.

The *French Horn*

In 1743, the Duke of Portland leased a tenement and smith's shop, formerly called the *White House* but then called the *French Horn*, to John Boddy of Chalfont St Peter, yeoman, for 21 years at a rent of £3 per year. The property included two acres of land on a common called Fulmer Heath or Gerrards Cross Common, fronting the Oxford to London road.[17] At the time of the Bulstrode sale in 1810, the *French Horn* was described as 'a house of great business, with roomy stables and other buildings, the principal part entirely new, immediately adjoining the high road from London to Oxford'. It was let to Moses Blinco, at the rent of £25 per year. Subsequent licensees included William Humber, 1820-21; Robert Lively Shepard, 1822; Thomas Green, 1823-8; and Elizabeth Yeowell, 1847. The *French Horn* had a particular role as a 'night house', where carters on the Oxford Road could rest their horses and themselves, before pressing on for London in the morning. In the early 20th century, there were repeated complaints to Gerrards Cross Parish Council about the inadequacy of the drains to cope with the numbers staying at the *French Horn*.

The *French Horn* was purchased by Weller's Amersham Brewery and was included in a Weller family settlement of 1862. Here it is described as the *French Horn Inn* with two adjoining messuages, used as a butcher's shop and a baker's shop, together with an acre of land at Gerrards Cross Common, Fulmer.[18] Later licensees included Francis Woodley, 1869; Ann Ridgeley, 1872; Thomas Shackell, 1877-95; J. Flexman, 1903; Charles Ivins, 1910; and George Penney, 1921. At the sale of Weller's Brewery in 1929, the *French Horn* was let to J.C. Channer at £50 per year. There was also a house and shop, rented by Mr Channer at £25 per year, and a further house and shop with an old bakehouse, let to Mrs Graham at £30 per year. The whole was bought by Messrs Benskins of Watford, who rebuilt the *French Horn* to the designs of local architect Robert G. Muir in 1946.

The *Packhorse Inn*

The earliest deeds to the *Packhorse Inn* date from 1707, when a brickmaker called Thomas Pyner purchased four acres of land for a new house

3 The *French Horn, c.*1908.

from Thomas Gascoigne, the then owner of the Orchehill estate. The land was part of a close or field of arable land called the Great Heath Field and was to be divided from the rest of the close by a ditch and bank at Pyner's cost. It was bounded by the remainder of the Great Heath Field on the north and east, by the common highway leading out of Jarrats Cross Heath to the town of Chalfont St Peter on the east, and by Jarrats Cross Heath on the south and west.[19] Thomas Pyner seems to have been a blacksmith as well as a brickmaker and beerseller. His successors at the *Packhorse* included Robert Cook, 1753-7; Hamock Shropshire, 1758-83; Leonard Addison, 1785-95; William Davis, 1796-7; Elisha Turner, 1798-9; Thomas Diton, 1800-8; William Piner, 1809-17; and William Hempsted, 1817-30. The row of cottages which once stood at the back of the *Packhorse Inn* had a

datestone inscribed 'Huntsman's Hall 1796'. This refers to the headquarters and kennels of the Old Berkeley Hunt, whose huntsman, Thomas Oldacre, lived here.

By 1826, the *Packhorse Inn* had been purchased by John and William Weller, brewers of Amersham. Their tenants at the *Packhorse Inn* included Thomas Rolfe, 1840, and Henry Cock, 1851. In an 1862 Weller family settlement the *Packhorse Inn* is described as situate at Gerrards Cross Heath, Chalfont St Peter, with five adjoining cottages, formerly known as the Huntsman's Hall, and four acres of land. Later licensees under Weller's Brewery included Ann Cock, 1869; Thomas Wren, 1872; Robert Chipps 1877-91; and John Bell, who combined the trade of publican with that of a blacksmith, and was a member of Gerrards Cross Parish Council from 1895-1907.

4   The *Packhorse Inn*, *c.*1955.

At the sale of Weller's Brewery and its tied houses in 1929, the *Packhorse Inn* was described as a well-known roadside inn with five bedrooms, let at a yearly rent of £100 to E. Bell, whose family had been in occupation for about 36 years. There was a row of five three-roomed brick and tile cottages, four let at 3s. per week and one at 4s. There was also two and a half acres of land with a road frontage of 175 feet, suitable for shop sites. The *Packhorse Inn* passed with Weller's other property to Benskin's Watford brewery. The new

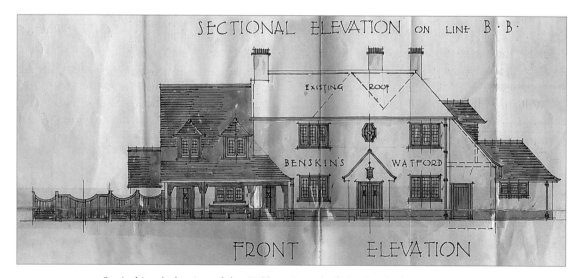

5   Architect's drawing of the *Packhorse Inn*, rebuilt by Benskin's Brewery, 1931.

owners made extensive alterations in 1931 to the designs of J.C.F. James ARIBA.

Beerhouses

There were other inns or, more properly, beerhouses around Gerrards Cross Common, but these would have served the locals, rather than travellers on the Oxford or Packhorse Roads. The *Fox and Hounds*, which probably took its name from the nearby meeting place of the Old Berkeley Hunt, stood opposite the *French Horn*. It is now known as the *Apple Tree*. The *Golden Cross* was situated between the Windsor Road and the *Bull Inn*, but went out of business in the late 19th century.

The Old Berkeley Hunt

A remarkable number of cottages and farmhouses around Gerrards Cross Common were converted in the late 18th and early 19th centuries into gentlemen's residences. This may well have been due to the establishment there of kennels for the Old Berkeley Hunt. The name of the hunt comes from the Earls of Berkeley who, during the 18th century, hunted a huge area from London in the east, to Berkeley Castle, Gloucestershire, in the west. Gerrards Cross became a popular meeting place for the hunt, perhaps because it was a large open space which the Gloucester coaches passed each day. The hunt was certainly meeting there by 1792, when the account book of Frederick Augustus, 5th Earl of Berkeley, records payments to 'William Hill, with the hounds at Gerrards Cross'. In 1793 the Earl paid over £200 for 'Thomas Oldaker's bills of wages and other expenses with the whippers in, helpers, hounds and horses at Gerrards Cross'.[20] New kennels and a house for the huntsman were built at the rear of the *Packhorse Inn*. The stone plaque reading 'Huntsman's Hall 1796' remained on the building until its demolition in the 1930s.

When the Earl of Berkeley gave up the mastership of the hunt about 1800, the Old Berkeley Hunt became a subscription pack, with the kennels remaining at Gerrards Cross. At this time certain English landowners opposed to fox hunting brought actions for trespass against masters of fox hounds. At a meeting of landowners in the Burnham and Stoke Hundreds in 1810, a motion was passed that 'hunting with foxhounds in this neighbourhood will be injurious to the value and enjoyment of property, and is wholly unsuitable to a country so near the metropolis'. The new owner of Bulstrode Park, the Duke of Somerset, and the owner of Chalfont Park, Thomas Hibbert, both signed the motion. This opposition did not discourage the eager huntsmen, who concentrated their activities in the well-drained valleys and luxuriant woodlands of south Buckinghamshire and the Chilterns.

The Old Berkeley's Huntsman, Thomas Oldacre, was probably considering retirement when, in 1818, he built a house, now known as Berkeley Cottage, on the corner of Mill Lane and East Common.[21] He died there in 1831 aged 80. Although the Old Berkeley Kennels moved first to Rickmansworth, and later to the great houses of successive masters, the Old Berkeley Hunt continued to meet at Gerrards Cross. Woodhill, the fine house on the Oxford Road belonging to Brasenose College, was evidently well-equipped as a hunting box. An 1829 valuation for the College described the very extensive stabling.[22] John Chantry, owner of Walters Croft House (now the Memorial Centre), was a particular enthusiast, and owned some very fine hunting horses. His well-known stud of hunters and his hunting gear were put up for auction, along with the contents of the house, in April 1843.[23] From 1869 to 1875, Oscar Blount of Orchehill House, and Leicester Hibbert of Chalfont Lodge were joint masters of the Old Berkeley Hunt. The Hon. William Le Poer Trench was also a keen huntsman, changing the name of Langley Lodge to St Hubert's, after the patron saint of hunting. Even as late as 1910, the compiler of a brochure advertising new houses on the Latchmoor Estate, stressed the advantages of the locality for the sportsman and mentioned the frequent meets of the Old Berkeley Foxhounds in the neighbourhood.

Bulstrode Park

Gerrards Cross may have been a place of importance on the Oxford Road before the advent of the Old Berkeley Hunt because of the proximity and stature of several nearby gentlemen's houses. The greatest of these was Bulstrode, an ancient estate situated south-west of the Oxford Road, which had been split in two at a very early date. The western half, situate in the parish of Hedgerley, was called Temple Bulstrode, having been given to the Knights Templar in the 13th century. A conveyance of Temple Bulstrode in 1670 included the Great Temple Field and referred to a moat, suggesting that the estate was centred on the present-day Moat Farm.[24] The eastern half was within a 123-acre detached portion of the parish of Upton, but, confusingly, it was called Hedgerley Bulstrode. The Victorian house called Bulstrode Park was built on the western boundary of this land.

The family who occupied Hedgerley Bulstrode from late medieval times took the surname Bulstrode and also accumulated property in several neighbouring parishes. In 1522, Margaret Bulstrode, widow, was assessed on land in Beaconsfield, Chalfont St Peter, Fulmer, Hedgerley Dean, Horton, Iver and Langley. Margaret's greatest wealth, however, was £100 worth of goods in Upton, presumably that part of the parish near Gerrards Cross.[25] Edward Bulstrode was Sheriff of Buckinghamshire in 1585. Henry Bulstrode is mentioned in the Chalfont St Peter court rolls in 1606; apparently he was keeping more sheep on Chalfont Heath (Gerrards Cross Common) than he was entitled to do.[27] Henry Bulstrode

was M.P. for Buckinghamshire in 1625 and was able to purchase the manor of Chalfont St Peter in 1626. He raised troops in the Chiltern Hundreds in support of Parliament at the commencement of the Civil War in 1642. Following the death of Henry Bulstrode, in 1643, his son Thomas sold Bulstrode and Chalfont St Peter to Thomas Gower. Most of the Bulstrode family are buried at Upton church, where there is a fine array of brasses and monuments to their memory.

Thomas Gower sold Chalfont St Peter to Richard Whitworth in 1650 and conveyed Bulstrode to Ambrose Bennett in 1652.[27] Bennett was immortalised by Thomas Ellwood in his account of a Quaker funeral at Amersham in 1665. Bennett was taking refreshment at the *Griffin Inn* when he saw the coffin of Edward Parrott, a wealthy Amersham maltster, pass by on its way to the Quaker burial ground. He drew his sword, dispersed the funeral procession, and left the coffin in the road, whilst the Quakers were conveyed to Aylesbury Gaol.[28]

When Ambrose Bennett died in 1675, Bulstrode was sold to George Jeffreys, later to become Lord Chief Justice. In 1686, Jeffreys was able to buy the neighbouring property of Temple Bulstrode, in the parish of Hedgerley, from Sir Roger Hill of Denham. George Jeffreys rebuilt the old house of the Bulstrodes and in 1686 had a surveyor produce a map of the improved property. It includes inset drawings of his new house, including an elevation of the wide south front with a central pediment. It also shows a road continuing the line of Bull Lane, across the Oxford Road, leading down to Hedgerly. Jeffreys had been a faithful servant of the hapless James II. When the King fled the country in 1688, Jeffreys too tried to escape to France, but he was captured and died in the Tower of London in 1689.

In 1692, George Jeffreys' family sold Bulstrode to Hans William Bentinck, a life-long friend and trusted adviser of the new king,

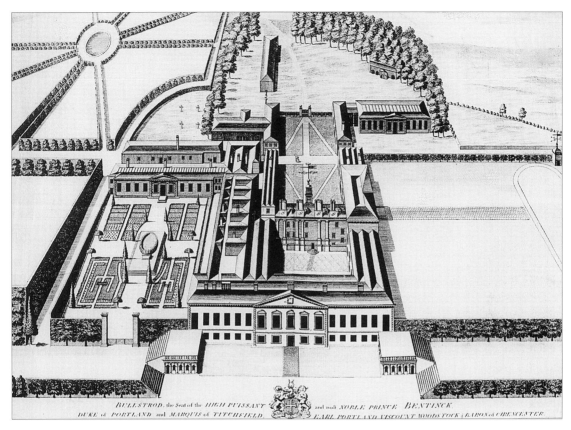

6 A 1730 engraving of Bulstrode, showing the house built for Judge Jeffreys in 1686.

William of Orange. Bentinck took a key roll in William's foreign policy initiatives and was created Earl of Portland in 1689. He evidently continued to develop Bulstrode for, in 1707, he obtained the consent of the leading freeholders in the district to the diversion of the road from Fulmer Heath to Hedgerly.[29] This may have fixed the line of the present Windsor Road and moved the crossroads with Oxford Road to its present site. It also enabled the Earl of Portland to extend the boundary of Bulstrode Park to include the British camp.

The Earl of Portland died in 1709 and was succeeded by his son Henry, who was created Duke of Portland by Queen Anne in 1716. The Dukes of Portland were content with their country estate until the 1740s, when the house was altered for William Bentinck,

2nd Duke of Portland. He employed the architect Stiff Leadbetter, who also worked on Shardeloes, Amersham, for William Drake. William Bentinck, 3rd Duke of Portland, Prime Minister in 1783 and again in 1807, commissioned James Wyatt to remodel the house in 1806-9. Contemporary drawings show Wyatt's new castellated wings alongside Jeffreys' classical-style house. A castellated gateway dating from this time survives to the west of the present house. William Bentinck died in 1809 before the rebuilding was completed.

The 4th Duke of Portland put Bulstrode on the market in 1810. It was eventually purchased by Edward Adolphus, 11th Duke of Somerset, but he failed to complete the rebuilding of the house. He even prepared a sale catalogue of the estate in 1814 but didn't proceed with

7 The entrance gate to the west of the present house is the only remnant of James Wyatt's remodelling of Bulstrode, 1806-9.

the sale.[30] The family used the house often enough for the Duke's daughter, Lady Charlotte, to have fond memories of the place. In 1839, she married William Blount, the Duke's agent at Bulstrode, and lived at Orchehill House on Packhorse Road. In 1841, Bulstrode was let to George Alexander Reid, son of a London brewer and a Colonel in the Life Guards.[31] He and his sisters lived at Bulstrode from 1841 until his death in 1852. He was elected M.P. for Windsor in 1845.

On the death of the Duke of Somerset in 1855, Bulstrode passed to Edward Adolphus, 12th Duke of Somerset. He gave the land on Fulmer Common for the building of St James's Church, Gerrards Cross, built in 1859. He was also responsible for the enclosure of Fulmer Heath in 1865, which enabled him and his successors to sell building plots on the south side of the Oxford Road. The Duke decided

to pull down the old house at Bulstrode and employed the architect, Benjamin Ferrey, to design a completely new house. Ferrey is best-known as a church architect, particularly for designing the new church at Penn Street in 1849. His new house at Bulstrode, started in 1861 and completed about 1870, bristles with towers, chimneys and gables.

When the 12th Duke of Somerset died in 1885, Bulstrode Park passed to his youngest daughter and co-heir, Lady Helen Guendolen, wife of Sir John William Ramsden, 5th Bart. On his death in 1914, Bulstrode was inherited by his only son, Sir John Frecheville Ramsden, 6th Bart, a businessman heavily involved in the Malayan rubber industry. He replanted the formal gardens and indulged his interest in rhododendrons. By the 1930s, however, Sir John Ramsden was in financial difficulties and his agents were marking out building plots on

8 Bulstrode Park, rebuilt 1861-70 by Benjamin Ferrey for the Duke of Somerset.

the Oxford and Windsor Roads. There was even a plan to turn Bulstrode Camp and part of the park into a golf course. In 1932, sales of the furniture, works of art and library were held, realising over £50,000. In November 1932, the house and 814 acres of land was auctioned and 43 of the 63 lots were sold, comprising 607 acres, bringing in a further £38,565.[32] Bulstrode Park itself, and some of the farmland, remained unsold. A major purchaser at the sale was Richmond Watson, whose Watson Investment Company was to develop the Camp Road and Dukes Wood estates.

During the Second World War, Bulstrode was occupied by the WAAFs and later by the RAF. In 1958, Sir John Ramsden sold the remaining furniture at Bulstrode Park and his land at Gerrards Cross was put up for auction. Bulstrode Park and 78 acres of land was sold to an organisation called the Bruderhof, or Society of Brothers, who hoped to turn it into an international conference centre.[33] Sir John Ramsden died later that year. In 1967, Bulstrode Park was purchased by the present owners, the Worldwide Evangelization for Christ, or WEC International.

Chalfont Park

Chalfont Park is the modern name for an ancient estate in Chalfont St Peter once called Brudenell's Manor, which took its name from the Brudenell family, resident there from the 15th century. In 1490, Drew Brudenell, of Chalfont St Peter, left 20s. in his will to the Fraternity of St Katherine in Amersham. In 1522, Edmund Brudenell was assessed on land in Chalfont St Peter valued at £20 and goods there worth £66 13s. 4d. When Edmund Brudenell died in 1538, his land in Chalfont St Peter passed to his daughter Elizabeth, wife of Robert

Drury. Drury also purchased the main manor of Chalfont St Peter, which had formerly belonged to Missenden Abbey. Brudenell's and Chalfont St Peter manors remained in the Drury family until 1626, when William Drury sold them to Henry Bulstrode of Hedgerley Bulstrode. During the remainder of the 17th century, Brudenell's was owned either by absentee landlords, or by those who held the estate for very brief periods. It is likely, therefore, that there was little investment in the estate and that the big house there remained somewhat old-fashioned.

It may have been the cost of Henry Bulstrode's prominent role in the English Civil War which caused his son, Thomas Bulstrode, to sell both Brudenell's, and the manor of Chalfont St Peter,

in 1645. Brudenell's eventually became the property of Dudley Rowse, Receiver General for Oxfordshire. When he died in 1678, owing large sums of money to the government, his estates, including Brudenell's, were seized by the Crown. In 1688, Brudenell's was given by the Crown to George Jeffreys, Lord Chief Justice, who had just built the new house at nearby Bulstrode Park.

Bulstrode and Brudenell's were not united for long, because John Lord Jeffreys sold Bulstrode to Henry Bentinck in 1692 and disposed of the manor of Brudenell's itself about 1695. The purchaser may have been the Duke of Leeds, who was party to the sale of the estate in 1707. The sale particulars described Brudenell's as a mansion house, garden, orchard, courtyard

9   Chalfont Park, built for Charles Churchill in the Gothic style, about 1755.

10 The southern entrance Lodge to Chalfont Park, demolished for the construction of the bypass in the 1960s.

and other yards, with dovehouse, barns, stables and other convenient outhousing, all moated round. The mansion house was rented to a tenant at the modest rent of £5 per annum. There was also a brick farmhouse, with the yard, granary, barns, stables and other convenient housing, which was let with 285 acres of land, to Robert Chirk, farmer, for £125 per annum. The whole property was valued at £3,325.[34] By 1714, John Wilkins, ironmonger, of the City of Westmister, had acquired Brudenell's. He probably lived in the old house whilst a tenant farmed the estate from the nearby brick house. In 1736, John Wilkins mortgaged Chalfont House to Lister Selman. A map and survey of the estate was made at this time, showing the 'capital mansion house' within the moat, and the 'new-built brick messuage' just to the south, right on the boundary of Chalfont St Peter with the detached part of Iver parish.[35]

In 1755, Lister Selman sold Chalfont House and the nearby farmhouse and land for £7,600 to the trustees of General Charles Churchill. They were acting on behalf of the General's son, Charles Churchill, who was a great nephew of John Churchill, 1st Duke of Marlborough. The younger Charles Churchill had married Maria, daughter of the Prime Minister, Robert Walpole. Walpole's fourth son, the author Horace Walpole, was a regular visitor to Chalfont House. It was he who introduced Charles Churchill to the architect, John Chute, who was to rebuild Chalfont House in the Gothic style, along the lines of Horace Walpole's famous house at Strawberry Hill, Twickenham. Capability Brown was employed to lay out the grounds. The moat and the farmhouse disappeared, but a weir across the River Misbourne produced an elegant lake to the south of the rebuilt house. The changes were radical enough to require the newly turnpiked Wendover to Oak End road to be moved westwards, away from Chalfont House. The lodges opposite Marsham Lane and Claydon Lane were built at either end of this diversion. They were demolished in the 1960s for the construction of the bypass.

In 1792, the trustees of General Charles Churchill promoted a private Act of Parliament which enabled them to sell Chalfont House. Accordingly, the estate was conveyed to Thomas Hibbert in 1794.[36] The Hibberts were originally from Cheshire but their wealth was in their plantations in Jamaica. Thomas Hibbert employed John Nash to make improvements to the exterior of Chalfont House and Humphry Repton to bring more farmland within the park. Thomas Hibbert died in 1819, when Chalfont House passed to his brother Robert Hibbert, also a Jamaica merchant and slave owner. On the death of Robert Hibbert in 1835, Chalfont House was inherited by his son, John Nembhard Hibbert, a veteran of the Battle of Waterloo, and Sheriff of Buckinghamshire in 1837. He made several alterations to the house, employing the architect Anthony Salvin. John Nembhard Hibbert built a new school in Chalfont St Peter and also provided the cottage hospital there in 1871. He died in 1886, aged 90. His executors sold the Chalfont House estate, extending to 1,037 acres, in 1888. Subsequent owners of the house were Captain Berton, John Bathurst Akroyd and Edward Mackay Edgar. Chalfont Park later became a hotel, then a technical centre for British Aluminium Company and is now occupied by the IT firm Citrix Systems.

Woodhill

Another early and significant gentleman's house on the Oxford Road was Woodhill. When William Drury sold Brudenell's Manor to Henry Bulstrode in 1626, the conveyance included much of the detached part of Iver parish, called Woodhill, which bounded on Chalfont Heath. In 1630, Henry Bulstrode sold Woodhill for £1,700 to Sir Sampson Dayrell,

whose son, Marmaduke, sold it on in 1642 to Sir William Acton. Sir William's daughter married Sir Thomas Whitmore, and their son William Whitmore sold it to Sarah, Duchess Dowager of Somerset. In 1679, the Duchess of Somerset gave Woodhill to Brasenose College, Oxford as an endowment for scholarships for four boys from Manchester School.[37] In April 1680, the College Bursar, Thomas Yates, drew up a plan of the new property, showing Chalfont Heath to the west, Hollow Lane (now Mill Lane) to the north-west, and the road from Chalfont to Uxbridge on the north-east. He included a sketch of Woodhill, the home of the college's principal tenant, Thomas Treadaway, who had a 21-year lease at £25 a year.[38] He also depicted Noke Mill and Oak End House, to the north of the Uxbridge Road. These were also in Iver parish and belonged to Henry Gould, who had a 21-year lease on part of the college land at the rent of £17 a year. Gould's house and mill have now disappeared, but they are recalled in the modern road name, Oak End Way.

For the next two hundred years, Brasenose College leased Woodhill House and the farmland to suitable tenants. The new occupant in 1777 was Elizabeth Hutchins, who came to agreements with the college to build a new barn and extend the house. Her new wing had a staircase and three rooms on the ground floor, one of them, measuring 25ft by 16ft, having a bow window. In 1784, however, Mrs Hutchins was selling the lease of Woodhill, on which it was claimed £900 had been spent. Her rent for the house was £108 a year.[39] The property was again advertised for sale in 1796. By this time the house was generally let separately from the farm. A valuation of 1829 gave the extent of the farmland as 212 acres, which were let to John Hayward Budd at £167 a year. One of the last Brasenose College tenants at Woodhill House was John Henry Saunders, a photographer, who died there in 1890. In 1894, Brasenose College finally sold

11 Woodhill, Oxford Road, 1907.

the freehold of Woodhill House, with 214 acres of land, to Colonel William Le Poer Trench, of St Hubert's, for £4,500.[40] After his death in 1920, a large portion of the Woodhill estate was bought by C.P. Lovell and divided into 81 building plots for large houses. Woodhill House itself fell into ruin and was demolished for redevelopment about 1970.

The Rancho

The most unusual of the gentleman's residences at Gerrards Cross was The Rancho, which stood south of the Oxford Road, opposite Woodhill. It was built in about 1862 by the author and adventurer Thomas Mayne Reid (1818-83). Reid had made a name for himself fighting with the Americans in the Mexican War, 1846-8. He returned to England in 1849, complete with war wound and the rank of Captain, and attempted to make a living writing fiction, mostly based on his own experiences. He married Elizabeth, daughter of George William Hyde, who claimed descent from the Earl of Clarendon, author of the *History of the Great Rebellion*. Reid himself wrote a fictional account of the Civil War in Buckinghamshire entitled *The White Gauntlet*. He also wrote

The Child Bride, probably based on his own courtship of Elizabeth, who was only 15 when they married in 1853.

Reid was initially very successful, particularly in writing adventure stories for boys, and had a loyal readership, both in England and in America. He invested the proceeds of his writing in a project to build a Mexican rancho at Gerrards Cross. In 1862, he leased 20 acres of the Woodhill estate from Brasenose College, and undertook to build a substantial house on the land.[41] He was his own architect and even supervised the brick-making on site. The house was flanked by two entrance lodges on the Oxford Road. Mayne Reid also built a row of nine cottages on Gerrards Cross Common, opposite the *French Horn*. The row included a public reading room and a house for a police constable. When Mayne Reid went bankrupt in 1866, The Rancho remained unfinished. He then left the district and for some years lived at Ross-on-Wye, in Herefordshire. The Rancho was bought from his creditors by Reid's neighbour, John Bramley-Moore of Langley Lodge, who bought the freehold of the land from Brasenose College in 1871, but left the house to decay.[42]

12   The Rancho, Oxford Road, a Mexican-style house built by the author, Thomas Mayne
Reid, in about 1862.

St Hubert's

The building of the large country house called
St Hubert's is connected with the enclosure of
the common land near Gerrards Cross, which
formed the northern limit of the parish of
Langley Marish. The common was bounded on
the east by an old farmstead called Prestwicks,
and on the west by a road to Gerrards Cross
which marked the boundary between Langley
Marish and Fulmer. Following the 1815
Enclosure Award for Langley Marish, two acres
of this common were allotted to Edmund Grove,
who had an old enclosure and a farmhouse
there, later known as Grove Cottages. By 1846,
a genteel house, called Langley Cottage or
Langley Lodge, had been built on the new
allotment, having a view over the eastern part
of Fulmer Common.[43] About 1863, this cottage
was purchased by John Bramley-Moore M.P., an
ambitious Liverpool merchant. He was Mayor of
Liverpool in 1848, Chairman of the Liverpool
Docks and Harbour Board and a director of the
London and North Western Railway Company.
He was Conservative M.P. for Maldon, 1854-9,
and for Lincoln, 1862-9.

John Bramley-Moore may have bought
Langley Lodge when the focus of his business
moved from Liverpool to London, but his
choice may also have been influenced by
the appointment in 1859 of his son, the
Rev. John William Bramley-Moore, as the
first vicar of Gerrards Cross. John Bramley-
Moore transformed Langley Lodge, completely
rebuilding the house with tall chimneys and
towers. The new house was supplied with
gas from his own gas works. There are date
stones on the coachman's cottage (1863) and
the stables (1866). In 1867 Bramley-Moore
bought the neighbouring house called The
Rancho from the creditors of Thomas Mayne
Reid, thereby extending his parkland as far
as the Oxford Road.[44] He adapted one of
The Rancho's entrance lodges on the Oxford
Road as a gatehouse for Langley Lodge. He
also acquired the row of nine houses on
East Common, which he renamed 'Bramley
Cottages'. When John Bramley-Moore died
at Brighton in 1886, he left an estate valued
at £167,815. He made various bequests to
local charities, including £500 towards a fund

13 Langley Lodge, later known as St Hubert's, rebuilt for John Bramley-Moore in about 1860.

to provide coal at Christmas to the poor of Gerrards Cross, to be known as the Bramley-Moore Coal Fund.

After the death of John Bramley-Moore, Langley Lodge and Bramley Cottages were purchased by William Le Poer Trench, a son of the 3rd Earl of Clancarty, who represented County Galway in the House of Commons, 1872-4. He had a colourful military career and rose to be a colonel in the Royal Engineers. The colonel was a keen sportsman and changed the name of his new estate at Gerrards Cross from Langley Lodge to St Hubert's. He even placed a large white stag over the porch, recalling the legend of St Hubert, who is said to have been converted after encountering a stag with a crucifix in its antlers. Such was the scale of sport he offered, that the Prince of Wales was a frequent visitor to St Hubert's. The colonel changed the name of the nine cottages on East Common from Bramley Cottages to St Hubert's Cottages. In 1894, William Le Poer Trench purchased the Woodhill estate, on the opposite side of the Oxford Road, from Brasenose College, Oxford.[45] He further extended the

grounds of Langley Lodge and in 1896 moved the road to Gerrards Cross, which passed his front door, further away to the south-west, creating the present-day St Hubert's Lane. A new carriage drive was laid out with an entrance lodge on St Hubert's Lane. Trench was the first Chairman of Gerrards Cross Parish Council, serving from 1895 until 1911. He died at St Hubert's in September 1920 and was buried at Fulmer church. His widow, Gladys Le Poer Trench, continued to live at St Hubert's until 1940 when the Triangle Secretarial College took over the house. She then moved to Prestwick Place and died in 1969.

Alderbourne Manor

Alderborne, also known as Nutting Grove, was an ancient estate in Langley Marish belonging, until the Dissolution of the Monasteries, to Ankerwycke Priory. In 1769, it was purchased by Benjamin Way as a suitable addition to the Denham Place estate.[46] In 1859, the Rev. Henry Hugh Way, Vicar of Henbury, Gloucestershire, resigned his living in favour of his eldest son,

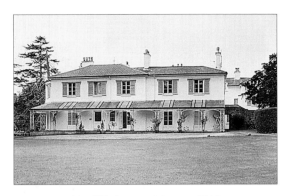

14   Alderbourne Manor, *c*.1930.

the Rev. John Hugh Way, and retired to live at Alderbourne with his youthful second wife. At this time, Alderbourne was still a working farm, run by his younger son, Lewis Way, who farmed the 300-acre estate with 20 labourers. The house was regarded as within the new ecclesiastical parish of Gerrards Cross, formed in 1859, and the Rev. Way always gave his address as Gerrards Cross. After his death, the house was inherited by the Rev. John Henry Way, who sold the Alderbourne Manor estate in 1907. The new owner, John Bell White, made alterations and additions to Alderbourne in 1907. He was High Sheriff of Buckinghamshire in 1918. Capt. White sold Alderbourne Manor in 1926 when it was described as having a lounge, hall, four reception rooms, billiard or music room and 20 principal and secondary bed and dressing rooms. There was an entrance lodge, garage and stabling with men's quarters, keepers' cottages, and a lake with a boat house.[47]

Berkeley Cottage
Berkeley Cottage was one of many small encroachments on Chalfont Heath tolerated or even encouraged by the lord of the manor in the 18th and 19th centuries. It was built in 1818 for Thomas Oldacre, the famous huntsman of the Old Berkeley Hunt, who died there in 1831 aged 80. The Old Berkeley Hunt kennels were at Huntsman's Hall, the cottages behind

the *Packhorse Inn*. Berkeley Cottage later became the property of George Healy, who lived at Latchmoor House and held nearby Woodhill Farm on lease from Brasenose College. When the house was sold by Miss Healey in 1906, it had a lounge with a large bay window, dining and morning rooms, three principal bedrooms, four back bedrooms, a coach house and two-stall stable.

The Memorial Centre
The three-storey house now occupied by Gerrards Cross Memorial Centre was formerly known as Walters Croft House, then Watercroft and later as Gerrards Cross Vicarage. Walters Croft was an ancient encroachment on Chalfont Heath, probably made by some enterprising but landless man who could use its natural resources to make a living cutting firewood, turning wooden articles, making pots, bricks and tiles, or simply grazing a few cattle. When he put up a cottage on the land, the locals may have turned a blind eye and the lord of the manor might have accepted the encroachment if the cottager paid him an annual rent. Walters Croft is first referred to in a mortgage of 1691 when Robert Egleton of Chalfont St Peter, yeoman, was mortgaging his newly built cottage on Chalfont Heath.[48] It is not clear whether this building was the forerunner of the Memorial Centre or indeed of Marsham Lodge, for both these grand houses were built on Walters Croft.

The cottage on Walters Croft was sold in 1723 to John Wilkins of Chalfont House.[49] He may have added the cottage to his extensive estate, or possibly rebuilt it for one of his family, or for a tenant. There is no sign of the house in the 18th-century surveys of Chalfont House, but architectural evidence suggests that the central part of the house dates from the late 18th century, and the wings and entrance lodges from the early 19th century. By 1830, Walters Croft House was the property of

15 Watercroft House, East Common, given in 1876 to the Vicar of St James's, Gerrards Cross, as the new Vicarage. Since 1947 it has accommodated the Gerrards Cross Memorial Centre.

John Chantry, a sporting gentleman, who was probably attracted to the site because the Old Berkeley Hunt met on the common in front of the house. In 1843, his very extensive collection of furniture, hunting horses and other effects was auctioned on the premises.[50] Walters Croft, or Watercroft as it became known, was later occupied by Josiah Cato.

By 1876, the house had been purchased by Louisa Reid, one of the two sisters who had financed the building of St James's Church. In November of that year, she gave the house to the Rev. William Addington Bathurst, Vicar of St James's Church, taking the old Vicarage by Latchmoor Pond in exchange. The Rev. Bathurst left Gerrards Cross in 1877, to be replaced by the Rev. Alfred Kennion. It was during the Rev. Kennion's illness in 1894 that the Vicarage was advertised to let. It had four reception rooms, eight bedrooms and good stabling.[51] Kennion was succeeded in 1895 by the Rev. John Matthew Glubb, who became a prominent member of the new Gerrards Cross Parish Council.

In 1922, the Rev. Glubb conveyed the stables and the north lodge of the Vicarage to a local committee for conversion into a village hall, as a memorial to the men of Gerrards Cross who had died in the Great War. The Memorial Hall comprised a billiard room, two meeting rooms and a kitchen, with a bowling green and tennis courts outside. In 1945, the Vicarage itself was purchased anonymously and presented to the village as a community centre. At the opening of the Gerrards Cross Memorial Centre in 1949, the benefactor was announced as Eric Lawrence Colston, of St Bernards, Oak End Way, son of Gerrards Cross's first schoolmaster, and a former managing director of the Hoover Company.

Marsham Lodge

Marsham Lodge was an elegant house which stood on the corner of Marsham Lane and East Common. An early occupant was William Henry Mason, later known as William Henry Pomeroy, who lived there about 1815. He was the son of Kender Mason, who owned Beel House, Amersham and had plantations in Montserrat, Antigua and Dominica. Pomeroy died at Chalfont St Giles in 1825. The next owner was George Spencer Smith, who leased Marsham Lodge in 1853 to Thomas William Thornes, son of the Rev. William Thornes, of Alderbury, Shropshire.[52] He lived there with his nephew and niece. Marsham Lodge was advertised for sale in June 1879, described as 'a freehold residence, with pleasure grounds and kitchen garden, fronting Gerrards Cross Common, containing nearly two acres; also about 21 acres of building and accommodation grass lands (nicely timbered)'.[53] Thomas William Thornes took the opportunity of the sale to buy the freehold. When he died in 1882, he left Marsham Lodge to his nephew, John Thomas William Jones, in trust for his niece, Mary Emma Jones. John Jones obviously had an interesting career, as he was a Lieutenant in the 43rd Light Infantry and later a captain in the Royal Canadian Rifles. He died at Marsham Lodge in 1885. When Mary Emma Jones died in 1906, she left Marsham Lodge to her cousin, Mary James, who made alterations and additions to the house in 1907 and again in 1913. She lived there into the 1920s. Marsham Lodge was demolished for redevelopment in about 1966.

Walpole House

Walpole House is one of a row of old cottages and farmhouses near Latchmoor Pond which were gentrified in the late 18th and early 19th centuries. It was originally known as Latchmoor House, but was briefly called Belle Vue in the late 19th century, and renamed Walpole

House about 1941. The earliest references to the house relate to William Beckwith, once the wealthy tenant of Fulmer Place, who moved to Latchmoor House about 1800. When he died in 1816, he left the house, with land in Latchmoor Field, to his daughter Elizabeth Smart. A later owner was James Wassell, the Beaconsfield surveyor, who came to live in Gerrards Cross about 1828. In 1840, his widow, Susan Wassell, occupied the property, which comprised the house, outhouses, lawn, garden, stack yard, orchard, paddock and meadow.[54] By 1851, Latchmoor House was occupied by George Healey, agent to the Duke of Somerset, who was farming 300 acres with 18 labourers. By 1871, George Healey was no longer the Duke's agent, but he was still farming a vast 750 acres, including Woodhill Farm, which he rented from Brasenose College, Oxford. By 1881, the house, now known as Belle Vue, was occupied by John Bromwich, a retired builder. He was succeeded by William Carter, a retired ribbon manufacturer, who also called the house Belle Vue.

By 1910, the house had reverted to its old name of Latchmoor House under the ownership of William Gurney, land agent, of Thorneycroft, Cokes Lane, Amersham. Gurney was probably related to George Healey, for William and his brother James Gurney were parties, with their cousin Henrietta Healey, to the purchase of the nearby Orchehill Estate in 1905. Latchmoor House was sold in 1912 to Herbert Brerton Baker, a professor at London University, who lived there until his death in 1935. Audrey Baker, his daughter, is one of Gerrards Cross's oldest residents and has recently published her research on Bulstrode Park. Latchmoor House was next occupied by the author and playwright, Edward O'Brien. About 1941, Jan Smit, a Dutch diamond merchant, took over the house. He renamed it Walpole House after HMS *Walpole*, which had been sent across the Channel to pick him up and ensure that his

16 Latchmoor House, now known as Walpole House, West Common, *c*.1900.

stock of industrial diamonds did not fall into enemy hands.

The Old Vicarage

When the farmhouse next to Walpole House was converted into a gentleman's residence, it was known as Latchmoor Cottage. When occupied by the vicar of Gerrards Cross it was naturally called the Vicarage. It was subsequently known simply as Latchmoor, but, since it has been divided, the major part has been called The Old Vicarage.

From about 1830, Latchmoor Cottage was the home of Tobias Gainsford, owner of extensive property in London including a house on Piccadilly. Gainsford's executors put the property on the market in 1846, when Latchmoor Cottage was described as

> in the immediate vicinity of Bulstrode and Denham Parks and the grounds of Chalfont House and surrounded by a highly respectable neighbourhood.

The front is stuccoed in imitation of stone, and the interior is most conveniently planned, and contains eight principal and secondary bed chambers, drawing and dining rooms, and library, a capital billiard room, housekeeper's room, kitchen, larder, brew house etc; the out offices are very complete, and comprise a coach house, three stall stable with loft over, tool houses etc; there is a large garden behind, well stocked with choice fruit trees, greenhouses and cucumber bed, and a rich meadow in the rear.[55]

When the new church at Gerrards Cross was consecrated in 1859, the first vicar, William John Bramley-Moore, came to live at Latchmoor Cottage. He was followed by the Rev. William A. Bathurst, who was vicar from 1869-77. In 1876, Louisa Reid, one of the founders of St James's Church, offered Watercroft House, East Common (now the Memorial Centre), as a more appropriate vicarage, and took Latchmoor Cottage in exchange. Latchmoor Cottage was later occupied by the landscape artist, Peter Graham, who grazed highland cattle on the

17   Latchmoor, the house in the centre (now known as the Old Vicarage), was the home of William J. Bramley-Moore, first Vicar of Gerrards Cross.

common and painted them through the glass doors of his studio. Graham was followed by a portrait painter, Frederick George Cullen, who made extensive alterations and additions to the house, then called Latchmoor, in 1900.[56] The Cullen family remained at Latchmoor until 1939, and it was only after the war that the house was divided.

Latchmoor House

The third house in the row by Latchmoor Pond was also a farmhouse, with a symmetrical brick façade, probably added in the early 19th century when it was first let to genteel tenants. In the 1830s the house belonged to Joseph Shackell,

who died in 1839. His widow Mary subsequently let the house to Robert Saunders. When the white-rendered house next door became the Vicarage, the name 'Latchmoor Cottage' was appropriated by the Shackells for their own house. Their tenant in the 1890s was Matthew Thomas Roe, a paper merchant, and Mrs Roe was still renting the house from the Shackell family in 1910. Latchmoor Cottage then became the home of Arthur Percival Saunders. In 1911, he employed the notable London architects, Forbes & Tate, to design a new north wing.[57] This was to make the house look very wide for its height and to destroy the symmetry of the building. Forbes & Tate went on to design two new houses on West Common, The Paddock House and Widenham House, as well as several houses in Oval Way. The renaming of Latchmoor House as Walpole House, by Jan Smit, enabled the occupants of Latchmoor Cottage to upgrade and call their home Latchmoor House, the name it retains in 2006.

Waterside

The fourth house in the row beside Latchmoor Pond, now called Waterside, was a small farmhouse, marked on the 1789 map of the Bulstrode estate. It was described in the Bulstrode sale catalogue of 1814 as a messuage, cowhouse and sheds, with a garden and two small meadows on Gerrards Cross Common, let to Richard Stevens as tenant at will. The next owner, John Kemp, did not live there and appears to have rebuilt it as a genteel house, called Latchmoor Villa. John Kemp was allotted a small plot of land near the house in 1846 on the enclosure of Latchmoor Field. In 1851, the house was occupied by Clara Haynes and her two servants. In about 1887, Thomas Samworth, formerly publican at the *Bull Hotel*, retired to Latchmoor Villa. Part of the land

behind the house was sold in 1906 to George Hampton for the development of Bulstrode Way. Thomas Samworth's widow, Emma Samworth, lived at Latchmoor Villa until 1920, and it was her daughter who renamed the house Waterside about 1924.

Woodbank

A gentleman's house with a rather different origin was Woodbank, later Raylands Mead, at the corner of Bull Lane and Oxford Road. It was here that the Earl of Portland founded a school for the sons of tenants on the Bulstrode estate and the neighbouring parishes about 1709. This was continued by the Dukes of Portland until the sale of Bulstrode in 1810, which included the schoolhouse and fields either side of Bull Lane in the occupation of John Appleton, schoolmaster, who was excused from rent. The schoolhouse then became a private residence, occupied by William Gaskell until his death in 1822, and then by his widow. From 1830, Woodbank was occupied by Stephen Cannon, and by his widow. By 1881, the house had been acquired by Fritz Oldaker,

18 Woodbank, Bull Lane, extended in 1906 for Sam Fay, General Manager of the Great Central Railway. The architect was William Eves ARIBA, of Uxbridge.

19 *Ethorpe Hotel*, Packhorse Road, 1947.

a retired saddler. His widow Hannah Oldaker continued to live there into the 1900s.

In 1906, Sam Fay, the General Manager of the Great Central Railway from 1899 to 1922, came to live at Woodbank. He had an extra wing built on the west side of the house.[58] Sam Fay remained at Woodbank until the 1920s. It was then purchased by Edward Gwynne Eardley-Wilmot, an early resident of Gerrards Cross, who previously lived at The Corner House, The Woodlands, from 1907. He renamed Woodbank Raylands Mead. The Eardley-Wilmots continued to own the house until the 1960s. It was demolished for redevelopment in 1980.

Ethorpe

The present-day *Ethorpe Hotel* was originally called Fernacre Cottage and was built in the early 19th century. It is shown on the 1840

Chalfont St Peter tithe map, when it was owned by Frederick Penny. The occupier was William Jones, the then lord of the manor of Chalfont St Peter, who died there in 1850. The house then had a succession of tenants including Henry Trumper, James Duncan, Dr James Bird, one time Physician General of Bombay, Colonel Alfred Tipping, and Lieutenant General John Haughton, formerly Acting Commissioner of Assam, who died in 1887. The next occupant was Alban E. Bellairs, a stockbroker and noted expert on the production of cider, who changed the name of the house to Ethorpe. The house was on the market in November 1906, when it was described as an 'old-fashioned residence, recently modernised, four reception rooms, 11 bedrooms and dressing rooms, stabling, gardens and meadow land of over 7 acres'.[59] It was purchased by Major General George Upton

Prior, a veteran of the Afghan and South African Wars. He represented Gerrards Cross on Eton Rural District Council and died at Ethorpe in 1919.

Ethorpe house was converted into a hotel in 1923, and Ethorpe Crescent was laid out in the former gardens. The garden fronting Packhorse Road was developed as the row of shops known as The Highway.

Orchehill House

Of all the old gentlemen's houses at Gerrards Cross, none has a longer pedigree or played a more crucial role in the development of the settlement than Orchehill House. This was an ancient farmhouse, first mentioned in the Chalfont St Peter court rolls in 1333 as ¾ virgate (about 90 acres) called 'the land of Didisworthe'.[60] A William Disworth is mentioned even as early as 1311. By 1401, Deedsworth Farm was occupied by John Tyler, whose surname was probably also his profession. He was a freeholder and paid the lord of the manor of Chalfont St Peter only 2s. per year chief rent, plus a pair of gloves worth 1d.[61] The latter payment must have been the remnant of some ancient feudal duty, similar to that owed by the lord of Farnham Royal, who had to bring a new glove to wear in supporting the monarch's arm at each coronation.

Deedsworth Farm was held successively by John Tyler, Robert Tyler, William Tyler, Richard Tyler and John Tyler before it was sold in 1561 by Henry Tyler to Edmund Hamshew (or Hampshire).[62] Henry Hamshew was fined at the Chalfont St Peter manor court in 1582 for letting his cattle into Latchmoor Field before the grain was removed. In 1613, John Hamshire sold Deedsworth Farm to Timothy Birchmoor. When Birchmoor died in 1625, his inquisition post mortem described his house as a capital messuage called Deedsworth Farm. Birchmoor's daughter Mary married Thomas Buckenham, who sold Deedsworth to Henry Gascoigne,

clerk, for £640 in 1664. It was then inherited by Thomas Gascoigne of London, grocer, who was living at Chalfont St Peter at the time of his death in 1711. In 1714, his executors sold Deedsworth Farm to the Earl of Portland, the new owner of Bulstrode.

Whilst Deedsworth Farm was in the hands of the Earls and Dukes of Portland, it was known as Gascoigne's Farm and later as Kiln Farm. It was leased in 1742 to William Riggs of Chalfont St Peter, brickmaker, suggesting that tiles and bricks were produced here over a period of centuries.[63] The brick kiln and pottery at the bottom of Marsham Lane survived until the building of 'Diss Park' about 1907. By 1791, the Duke of Portland was selling off some of the property around Bulstrode. In that year, Deedsworth Farm, then known as Kiln Farm, and comprising 114 acres, was conveyed to Francis Peter Mallet of Langley Marish.[64] Francis Peter Mallet was Sheriff of Buckinghamshire in 1793. It was probably during Mallet's ownership that the farmhouse was rebuilt as a gentleman's residence and renamed Orchard Hill. When Francis Peter Mallet died in 1799, the *Gentleman's Magazine* described him as 'an eminent cabinet maker in Clerkenwell'.[65] Mallet's successor was Thomas Ludbey, formerly of Harley Street, London. He died in 1819 but his widow remained in occupation of the house until her death in 1841.

In 1842, the Rev. Thomas Ludbey put the 135-acre Orchard Hill estate on the market. An elaborate map of the estate was produced with an inset drawing of the house.[66] The sale particulars stressed its advantageous position, overlooking the grounds of Chalfont Park without the expense of their maintenance. The house comprised a drawing room and parlour, each 27ft, with bow windows, library, breakfast room and ten bedrooms. The Orchard Hill estate would suit a 'sporting man or a retiring merchant'. Packs of hounds met in

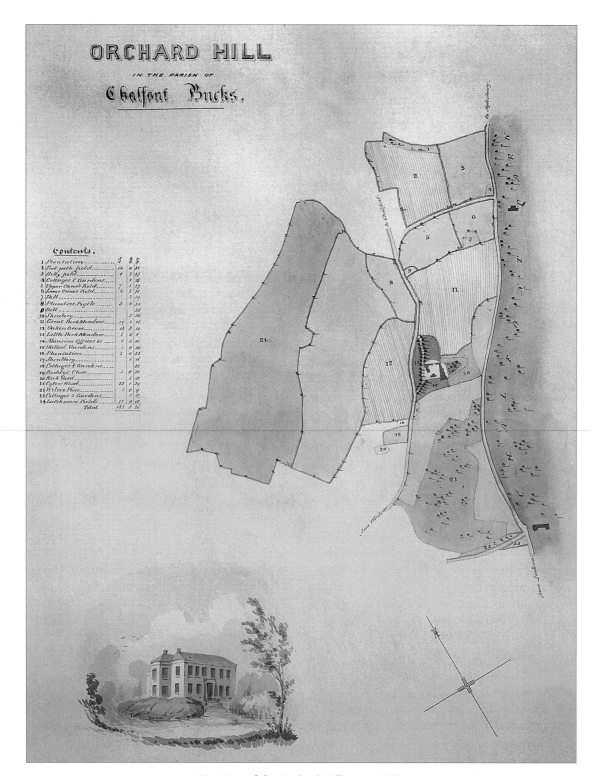

20 Map of the Orchard Hill estate, 1842.

21   Orchehill House, *c.*1900. The house now accommodates St Mary's School.

the vicinity and there was 'ample game for amusement'. It was also pointed out that the house was only 20 miles from London and eight miles from the new railway station at Slough.[67] No purchaser was found at the first sale but the property was eventually purchased by the trustees of the marriage settlement of William Blount and his wife Lady Charlotte, daughter of the Duke of Somerset, who had married in 1839.

Lady Charlotte had been a regular visitor to the family home at Bulstrode. It must have been a great surprise, however, when she announced her intention of marrying William Blount, the agent on the Bulstrode estate. Blount was born in 1799, the son of William Blount of Orleton, Herefordshire. He had married, in 1821, Eliza, youngest daughter of Thomas Wright Esq., of Fitzwalters, Essex, so Lady Charlotte was his second wife. Their new house, now called Orchehill, was greatly extended and embellished so that it resembled a Gothic mansion, bearing comparison with nearby Chalfont Park. In 1846, William Blount paid for the straightening

of Packhorse Road for 855 yards between Fernacre Cottage (later to become the *Ethorpe Hotel*) and Austenwood Common. The old road was taken into his garden.[68] Orchehill House was now approached by three driveways from newly built lodges on Oxford Road, Lower Road and Packhorse Road. Two of these lodges survive, although the lodge on Packhorse Road was demolished for redevelopment as recently as 2005.

William Blount's son, Oscar, born in 1842, was joint master of the Old Berkeley Hunt with Leicester Hibbert of Chalfont Lodge from 1869 to 1875. William Blount died in 1885 and Lady Charlotte in 1889. Oscar Blount left Orchehill in 1891, when the house was let to George Thornton. Orchehill was soon vacant again, for it was advertised to let in July 1893 as a 'lovely old historical mansion with a large number of magnificent reception rooms (all 40ft to 50ft in length)' on which over £20,000 had recently been spent.[69] It was then sub-let to John Ashton Cross, who later lived at Alderbourne Manor. In 1905, anticipating

22 Orchehill House was approached by three driveways from lodges on Oxford Road, Lower Road and Packhorse Road. This lodge on Packhorse Road was demolished in 2005.

the opening of the railway to Gerrards Cross, Oscar Blount and his wife, Mary Francis, sold the Orchehill House and 193 acres of land to Henrietta Healey for £29,000.[70] Henrietta Healey was the cousin of James and William Gurney, the local estate agents who were to develop the whole of the Orchehill estate over the next few years. Mr Thornton gave up his lease on Orchehill House, which was later let to Charles James Hurst and William Lloyd Brown Davies. In 1921, the Gurneys sold Orchehill House for £7,500 to George Sharp who lived there until the Second World War. In 1942, George Sharp sold the house to the Fidelity Trust who in 1945 conveyed it to St Mary's School, the present occupants.

The Enclosure of Latchmoor Field

William Blount of Orchehill House was the main promoter of the enclosure of Latchmoor Field in 1846. Latchmoor Field was a remnant of one of Chalfont St Peter's common fields, where local farmers had strips of cultivated land intermixed with those of their neighbours

and where a system of rotation of crops was practised. The system had long since broken down in most of these common fields and the farmers had reallocated the strips into discrete blocks of land. That the same process had not taken place at Latchmoor suggests a reluctance on the part of at least one proprietor to abandon the traditional mode of arable farming.

William Blount had 22 acres of land dispersed around Latchmoor Field, whilst John Nembhard Hibbert of Chalfont Park, owner of the farm later known as The Priory, had 14 strips. Blount received the largest allotment, situated at the bottom of the field, near Latchmoor Pond. Hibbert received the next largest portion, 15 acres to the north of Blount's allotment. A nine-acre allotment was given to Eleanor Peake, widow of Thomas Peake, the former owner of Maltmans Green Farm. William Jones, as lord of the manor of Chalfont St Peter, received a small allotment at the north, or top of the field. Other beneficiaries were George Spencer Smith, owner of Marsham Lodge, and John Kemp, who held the farmhouse by Latchmoor Pond, now known as Waterside. Enclosure commissioners were empowered to sanction exchanges of land after the allotments had been made. In a subsequent exchange, William Blount not only gained control of Hibbert's and Peake's allotments in Latchmoor Field, but also consolidated his holding by acquiring The Priory Farm.[71]

The enclosure of Latchmoor Field was of vital importance to the development of Gerrards Cross because it brought the majority of the land north of Gerrards Cross Common into single ownership. William Blount was able to build a carriage drive across the former open field. More significantly, in 1905, when Oscar Blount sold Orchehill to James and William Gurney, a huge block of development land next to the new railway station came into the hands of two hungry and ambitious estate agents.

Two

The Parish of St James, Gerrards Cross

In July 1841, the Duke of Somerset let the house at Bulstrode Park to Col George Alexander Reid, of the 2nd Lifeguards, for the modest rent of £157 per year.[1] Reid was the son of the wealthy brewer, Andrew Reid, of Liquor Pond Street, London and Lion's Down, East Barnet, who had died in April 1841. In 1845, George Alexander Reid became M.P. for Windsor. Although he maintained a large house in London, he and his two unmarried sisters lived part of each year at Bulstrode Park. He renewed the lease of Bulstrode Park in 1848 at £690 per year, this time taking more of the farmland and sporting rights.[2] In his will of 1852, he made his twin sister, Anna Maria, his sole executrix, and left £5,000 to his younger sister, Louisa. After their brother's death, the two sisters rented The Pickeridge, Fulmer, a much smaller house on the Bulstrode estate, but outside Gerrards Cross.

Anna Maria and Louisa Reid contrived a plan to honour their late brother's memory by building a church at Gerrards Cross. In 1856, Louisa Reid wrote to the Duke of Somerset, requesting a site for the church on Fulmer Common. The Duke consulted his agent about the legality of granting a piece of common land but was advised that a grant for a church would be legitimate. Indeed the agent agreed with Miss Reid that the building of a church 'would be decidedly of advantage to your property, as adding respectability in that locality'.[3] Plans were drawn up by the architect, William Tite, who had designed the Royal Exchange in 1844

and was a friend of the Reid family. The new church at Gerrards Cross was in the then highly unusual classical style and received a very full account in *The Builder*.[4] It was consecrated on 30 August 1859.

In promoting the case for the new church, it was claimed that householders near Gerrards Cross had to travel seven miles to church at Upton cum Chalvey, six miles to Langley Marish, six miles to Iver, two miles to Fulmer and two-and-a-quarter miles to Chalfont St Peter. The new ecclesiastical parish of Gerrards Cross was to comprise parts of these five parishes totalling 954 acres, with 109 dwelling houses and a supposed population of 545.[5] The original boundaries took no account of roads, streams and field boundaries, but were marked on the map using straight lines to connect important houses like Bulstrode Park, Orchehill House and Alderbourne, which were to be within the new parish of St James. Two of the original boundary stones, each marked G.C. 1860, survive on Bull Lane and Packhorse Road.

The Enclosure of Fulmer Heath
Until the building of St James's Church in 1859, there were no buildings on the south side of the Oxford Road between the *French Horn* and the *Bull Inn*. This, like Gerrards Cross Common on the north side of the road, was common land, and was known to the locals as Fulmer Common or Fulmer Heath. The cattle and sheep belonging to farmers in Chalfont St

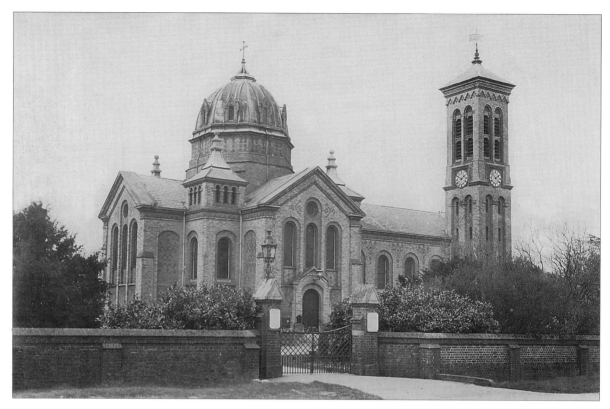

23 St James's Church, *c*.1900.

Peter and Fulmer must have grazed together on the two commons and crossed the Oxford Road at will. This situation was changed by the 1865 Fulmer Enclosure Act, which enabled the Duke of Somerset to enclose not only Fulmer Common, but also Stoke Common in the south of the parish. All the proprietors of farms in Fulmer parish received allotments of common in proportion to their existing land. The Duke of Somerset, who owned 853 acres of enclosed land, received allotments of common totalling 138 acres. He received a further 21 acres in lieu of his manorial rights over the commons. As the principal promoter of the enclosure, he was allotted parcels of land convenient to himself, most of which were to the east of Bulstrode Park, either side of the Windsor Road, and behind the *French Horn* inn.[6] The enclosure of Fulmer

Heath enabled the Duke of Somerset to sell building plots along the Oxford Road even before the railway from Gerrards Cross to London was opened in 1906.

Gerrards Cross Church of England School
Soon after the opening of St James's Church, the energetic new vicar, the Rev. John William Bramley-Moore, no doubt encouraged by the Misses Reid, sought subscriptions for a school. Gerrards Cross Church of England School was built in 1861. It occupied half an acre of land which was taken from Gerrards Cross Common by permission of the Rev. E. Moore as lord of the manor of Chalfont St Peter. Numbers attending rose after the opening of the railway in 1906. Consequently, the school was extended in 1913, with Johnson & Boddy, architects, working with Frank Green, builder.[7] In 1920,

24   Gerrards Cross Church of England School, East Common, built 1861, demolished 1971.

Charles E. Colston resigned as headmaster of the school, having served from 1880. He was also Clerk to Gerrards Cross Parish Council from its inception in 1895 until his resignation in January 1928. When the school moved to new premises at Moreland Drive in 1968, the original school remained empty whilst alternative uses were sought. The buildings were eventually demolished in 1971, and Colston Court flats were built on the site in 1974.

The Aged Pilgrims' Home

It was probably due to the influence of Miss Reid that the Aged Pilgrims' Home was built on East Common in 1874. It was erected by the Aged Pilgrims' Friend Society, which had been founded in 1807 to provide Christians, of any Protestant denomination, with a small pension to avoid poverty in old age. The society not only arranged the payment of these pensions but set up residential homes, the first being in Camberwell in 1834. The home at Gerrards Cross originally accommodated 15 old people. It was endowed with £250 a year by Sir John Wallis Alexander, 4th Bart, in memory of his brother, Sir William John Alexander, 3rd Bart, Attorney General to the Prince of Wales, who died in 1873. The buildings were designed by Habershon & Pite. The complex has now been converted into eight units, known as 'Hartley Court'.

Development around the Common

Until the arrival of the railway the Common contained most of the ordinary houses of the parish. After the building of the church a number of new houses were built and others modified. The 1912 valuations of the

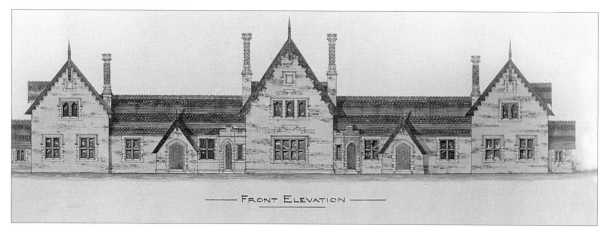

—— FRONT ELEVATION ——

25 Architects' drawing of the Aged Pilgrims' Home, Gerrards Cross, designed by Habershon & Pite, 1874.

group of houses near Latchmore Pond show that they still dominated the area. Latchmoor Villa (now known as Waterside) was valued at £800. Latchmoor Cottage (now known as Latchmoor House) was more substantial, but the valuation is not given. Latchmoor, which had served briefly as the vicarage, was the largest house valued at £2,100. Latchmoor House (now known as Walpole House) was valued at £1,280. All had considerable areas

of land not included in these figures. Between them and the *Packhorse Inn* there were six houses. The largest of these was Buena Vista, later occupied by Adelaide Healy, widow of the Bulstrode agent, George Healy. Then there were Ivy Cottages, valued at £200 and £240, owned in 1912 by James Langstone, who lived in one of them. Next were Heath Cottages, with an 1830 datestone, owned in 1912 by H.J. Smith of Hillingdon, and valued at £150

26 St Hubert's Cottages, East Common, *c*.1930.

each. In 1880, four cottages named Broom Cottages were built, also owned by Smith in 1912, and valued at £150 each.

The houses on the east side of the Common were split into two by Mill Lane. To its north lay Marsham Lodge and the Vicarage, with its two lodges. Both were substantial houses and in 1912 were valued with their land at £3,750 and £5,500 respectively. South of Mill Lane, Berkeley Cottage (£2,300) and Grove House were two fairly substantial buildings. They were followed by the semi-detached Oak Cottages (valued at £400 and £450) and a terrace of six cottages called Common View (most valued at £125). Next was the more substantial Heatherside (£500) and then a pair of semi-detached cottages called 'Gerrards Cross Cottage' and 'The Cot' (£200), before St Hubert's Cottages, valued at £128 each. Finally there were two small cottages near to the *Fox and Hounds* beerhouse.

Across the Oxford Road, near its junction with the Fulmer Road, Brasenose College had built Four Lane End, or Woodhill Cottages, valued in 1912 at £120, with land valued at £51. Again in the final quarter of the century, two new cottages were built in Fulmer Road, valued at £195 with land at £50. They were owned in 1912 by an Uxbridge solicitor.

By 1876, development between the Windsor Road and the *Bull Hotel* was limited to the old *Golden Cross* beerhouse and some cottages belonging to the Bulstrode estate. These were the four cottages later called New Pond Cottages (valued at £170 in 1912) and, a little further north, Woodbank Cottages (most valued at £150). Between 1876 and 1898 four major houses were built near to the Windsor Road junction. The largest was Heathfield, occupied in 1887 by Capt. F.G. Munns, and valued at £1,800 in 1912. Nearer the *Bull Inn* were two semi-detached houses, Elmleigh, occupied by George Ratcliff, a parish councillor in 1895, valued at £802, and Fernhurst, occupied by Miss Edith

Francis in 1899 and valued at £620. Then came another detached house called The Coppice, occupied by Miss Stephens. These were certainly the sort of houses and respectable people the Misses Reid had hoped to attract to Gerrards Cross. All of these houses, at one stage or other, had servants. No development was to occur on this side of the Oxford Road before 1898 but, shortly afterwards, the Bulstrode Estate built a row of four cottages called Lochnagar, Ashburton, Gorse Cottage and Mitford. They were valued at £360-75 each in 1912. One of the cottages was occupied by Henry Cocks, the builder, whose yard was nearer the *Bull Inn*.

In 1876, on the opposite side of the Oxford Road to the *Bull Inn*, stood the Post Office and an old smithy. Behind them on the Common were West End Cottages, belonging to the Bulstrode Estate. In 1912, these were valued at £165, £205 and £225. Nearer Latchmoor Pond were two cottages later to be called Devon Cottages.

The prospect of the development of genteel houses on the Common may have been limited by the availability of land. Landowners were conscious of the growth in demand for large houses in their own grounds, which occurred in the Chilterns towards the end of the 19th century. This was certainly true in the case of the executors of Hugh Budgen Peake, who, in July 1891, auctioned 27 acres on the east side of Bull Lane, near the Common, in seven lots, each 'suitable for the erection of a Gentleman's Country Residence'. In the event these seven houses were not built, so perhaps the demand was less than had been anticipated.

Gerrards Cross Parish Council

Following the Local Government Act of 1894, English parishes were to have elected parish councils. Gerrards Cross, which was only an ecclesiastical parish, took the opportunity to claim independence from the five surrounding civil parishes. When the new Gerrards Cross

27   Heatherside and Gerrards Cross Cottage, East Common, *c.*1900.

Parish Council met for the first time on the 25 November 1895, a vote of thanks was given to Mr Witham, the former agent on the Bulstrode Estate, 'for the pains he had taken in obtaining the new Parish'. Although he was abroad at the time, Col William Le Poer Trench, of St Hubert's, was elected Chairman, and Abram Ennis Bellairs, of Ethorpe, was made Vice Chairman. Other members were George Maltby Nicholls, of Park House; William Arnold, boot maker, East Common; John Bell of the *Packhorse Inn*; George Ratcliff and James Clark.

One of the first concerns of the new council was to review the somewhat arbitrary boundaries inherited from the ecclesiastical parish. New boundary stones were commissioned, but were not put in place until 1905. The boundaries were still made up of straight lines contrived in a drawing office in 1860. This was to prove a great problem after the coming of the railway, when several of the new houses, built on plots following the lie of the land, were found to be half in Gerrards Cross and half in Chalfont St Peter. It was also a problem for the census enumerators, who had to provide figures for both civil and ecclesiastical parishes. The issue was not resolved until 1934 when boundaries across the nation were reviewed. Detailed changes were made to the Gerrards Cross boundary so that it followed road, railway and property boundaries.

Three

The People of Gerrards Cross, 1851-1901

For the 19th-century census takers the basic unit was the civil parish, although figures were published for ecclesiastical parishes where these differed from the civil ones. For census enumerators, probably working without maps, this caused problems. In the case of Gerrards Cross this is reflected in the imprecise way in which households were allocated to the new area. This was not an ancient parish where beating the bounds and the operation of the poor laws might have meant there would have been little uncertainty. In consequence, although figures for the new parish were published from 1871, some caution needs to given to them. The story they reveal is a simple one, the number counted on census night being sensitive to the presence or absence of the principals of the main houses.

The Population of Gerrards Cross 1851-1901		
1851	560	
1861	560	
1871	630	(126 houses, 8 empty)
1881	640	
1891	630	
1901	552	(136 houses)

The increase in the population from 1851 to 1871 is largely accounted for by the 47 people at Bulstrode Park at the latter date, when the Duke of Somerset was, uniquely for a census date, in residence. The rise could also have been linked to the Duke's decision to rebuild Bulstrode Park. Certainly bricklayers and brickmakers feature prominently in the population between 1851 and 1871. The most

definitive fall in population was between 1891 and 1901, just at the time the railway was being discussed.

Four trends emerge from a study of the census enumerators' books: the replacement of agriculture with estate work as the major occupation, a growth in the number of people with claims to gentility, increased interconnection with London, and an influx of those born further afield. The figures do suggest that Miss Reid was right in advising the Duke in 1856 that building a church would encourage a better class of resident.

The Aristocracy

At the top of Gerrards Cross society was the aristocracy, with houses in London and several elsewhere. They would expect to play a major role in the London season and often in politics. According to Oscar Blount, the Duke of Somerset was only in residence at Bulstrode Park at Easter and Whitsun, and then again from the end of the London season to the middle of September, when he departed for his house at Maiden Bradley in Wiltshire. After the Duke's death in 1885, the house came into the possession of Sir John Ramsden. As an M.P. and one time Under Secretary for War, he too would spend most of his time in London.

The Gentry

The county gentry were less likely to play a major role in London society and would typically be found in their major residences.

The Blounts at Orchehill, the Hibberts at Chalfont Park and the Ways at Alderbourne were all typical of this group. Another group especially important in the Home Counties were those who had retired from foreign service in the Army or the Indian Service. This group, without a major stake in land, were likely to rent properties for a relatively short period. Colonel Reid, who rented Bulstrode Park, Colonel Tipping and Generals Haughton and Prior at Ethorpe were good examples of such gentry. Those who were not too old might be drawn to the area for country sports, such as Colonel Le Poer Trench at St Hubert's. Ease of access to London would have been very important to this group as, like the aristocracy, they would have had positions of importance in the government and society to maintain.

Below the minor gentry were the upper middle classes who would generally be retired or semi-retired. Occasional access to the capital would be important and, like those from the foreign service, they would often rent properties. They would have had few links with Gerrards Cross before arrival. Most would either have been born in the capital or at a considerable distance from it. They would generally maintain smaller households than the gentry proper, but they would certainly have employed servants. A surprisingly large proportion of this group were widows or maiden ladies. For them, the ease with which relations from London could visit was as important as their own journeys to London. Clean air and pleasant vistas would be important. Below the middle classes, but sharing some of their characteristics, were a few retired artisans from London who would be unlikely to keep a servant. Typical of these was Henry Langstone, a retired Metropolitan Police Inspector, living at Rose Cottage, East Common, in 1891.

Agriculture
Within the agricultural sector society was equally divided. The major farmers would either

come from families with a long tradition in the area, like the Healeys, or as major tenant farmers would have moved from a distance into the area. As a group they, and the estate managers of the gentry, were distinct from farm bailiffs who would often have risen from among the agricultural labourers. The latter and their wives were likely to have spent most of their lives in the area, albeit not necessarily in the same parish.

Most of the land around Gerrards Cross was held by the major estates. This land was controlled by stewards or land agents, like Charles Hilton of Oak End, farm bailiff and later agent to John Nembhard Hibbert, of Chalfont Park, from 1851–87. The most powerful were the agents of the Duke of Somerset, at Bulstrode. William Blount was the agent from 1827–39, but he resigned on his marriage to the Duke's daughter, Lady Charlotte. George Healey held the position from 1842–63. In 1861, he was living at Latchmoor House, farming 500 acres, and employing two domestic servants and 22 farm labourers. John Henry Witham was agent from 1863 to 1877, living at Ivy House, Hedgerley Lane. John Charles King then held the position until 1885. Robert Baty was agent from 1885 to 1941. He was prosperous enough in 1891 to keep a servant and had two by 1901. Baty continued to rise in society, moving from Ivy House to Park House, on the corner of Hedgerley Lane, about 1920. Park House was lot 35 in the 1932 sale of the Bulstrode estate. It comprised drawing room, dining room and morning room, each with a bay window, and five bedrooms, three of which had bay windows. It was sold for £1,200.[1]

Below the stewards were the farm bailiffs. Henry Dolan employed George Marshall as bailiff at Marsham Farm in 1881. He employed 11 labourers although some of these may have worked at the brick kiln on the property. The Rev. Way of Alderbourne employed a succession of bailiffs to manage Alderbourne

Farm, including George Lovelock in 1881, and William Harris in 1891. At St Hubert's the emphasis on sport was reflected in the promotion of the gamekeeper in 1891 to estate bailiff by 1901.

With the dominance of the major estates, few farmers were freeholders, which may explain why no son succeeded his father as a farmer in this period. Domestic servants were few in farming households. From 1847 to 1863, the lower gardens at Bulstrode seem to have been let as a market garden to William Hook.[2] He employed six labourers there in 1851, two of whom lived in. He had retired by 1871, when he was 82 and living at Vine Cottage, Windsor Road, with his wife, daughter, granddaughter and one servant.

Agricultural Labourers 1851–1901
The farm labourers tended to live in cottages dispersed around the big estates. Unlike the agents and large tenant farmers, they and their wives were likely to have spent their whole lives in the area, but not necessarily in the same parish. There was a marked decline in the percentage of the population involved in farming from 1851 to 1901, reflecting not only a national trend to more efficient farming but also a change in emphasis from agriculture to country sports on the part of the major proprietors. Many who would have described themselves as agricultural labourers found positions as gardeners as the number of genteel houses increased.

Shopkeepers
The tradesmen, shopkeepers, publicans and others who might be thought of as higher artisans were another group likely to have

moved into Gerrards Cross from a distance. Their entrepreneurial instincts might have suggested to them that this was an area of growing affluence and the new church would have created a powerful image. Certainly, some of this group made financial if not social progress.

The Post Office, situated opposite the *Bull Inn*, was perhaps the most important of the local facilities. This was run until 1836 by William Hunt, and then by his widow, Elizabeth, who was born locally and was postmistress in 1851. In 1853 Robert Matthews took over, combining the roll of postmaster with the trade of a tailor. He had been born in Greenwich. He was succeeded in 1864 by William Robert Matthews, who had been born locally in 1834 but whose wife was from Bloomsbury. By 1871 he was employing one man and a boy but neither lived in. By 1881 his son, Arthur Frederick, was shown as an assistant postmaster. Arthur Matthews was the postmaster by 1887 and continued to combine the post with the trade of a tailor. He built a new post office and tailor's shop on the corner of Marsham Way in 1907, and continued as postmaster until 1913, when the new Post Office was opened. Matthews was not appointed as the new postmaster, causing a storm of protest locally.

There were two shops next to the *French Horn*, a baker's shop occupied by the Wood family and a butcher's shop, run by Richard Scott. James Wood was born in Kent and had moved to Gerrards Cross by 1851. He was trading as a grocer and baker, employing a journeyman and a domestic servant to assist his wife with their six children. In 1861 he was employing a baker's lad. By 1881 his

Agricultural Labourers as per cent of Population						
	1851 %	1861 %	1871 %	1881 %	1891 %	1901 %
Male agricultural labourers	47.5	27.5	26.7	19.6	22.4	9.5
Male labourers	3.2	14.4	12.8	9.5	4.2	4.8

28 The Old Post Office, otherwise known as Flint Cottage, opposite the *Bull Inn*, 1913.

widow Jane Wood was running the grocery and baker's business with her son, Alfred, and one other baker. Alfred Wood moved the business to a new shop on the corner of Station Parade and Oak End Way in 1908, but evidently over-reached himself, for the premises were in different hands by 1910. Richard Scott was born in High Wycombe and was running the butcher's shop by 1861. He and his wife had had at least five children by 1871, but at no stage did his business employ a live-in assistant or, indeed, any of his sons. One was a bricklayer and two were joiners. By 1881 he had made enough money to move to a new shop on East Common, but he died about 1891 with no successor in the business. Henry J. Bonsey, who had started business in Scott's old shop next to the *French Horn*, now took over the new premises at East Common. Like Scott he never had a live-in assistant, although by

1891 there was one domestic servant in the household and in 1901, by which time his wife had died, there were two such servants. By 1907 Bonsey was wealthy enough to set up his son Frederick in business as a butcher in Station Road.

Whilst these shopkeeping families may have benefited from the construction of the church and the progress to gentility, none had been newly attracted to Gerrards Cross. In 1861, however, John Henry Witham, who was to take several roles in the area, a linen draper and bookseller, was living in Grove House, East Common. He was born in High Wycombe but his wife had been born in Holborn. How long his business survived is not clear, but by 1871 he had become the local agent for the Duke of Somerset and was living at Ivy House, Hedgerley Lane. One trader who may have moved some distance was Thomas Penny, draper, born in Totnes, with a wife born in Suffolk.

They had evidently spent time in London as several of their children had been born in Paddington between 1860 and 1865. They lived in Oak Cottage, also on East Common, next door to John Edwards Drew, another draper. Drew was not at home on census night in 1871, but his children were there with their governess and a domestic servant. Like Penny, his children had been born in Paddington, so the two may have been in partnership, or one working for the other. Penny remained in business until about 1891, although in that census he describes himself as retired.

Perhaps the most dramatic climb in status was that experienced by William Payne. In 1892 his daughter married a labourer, Leonard Charles Rickard. In 1901, then aged 37, he was resident in St Hubert's Cottages and described as a cycle maker. By 1907 he was building a new cycle shop on Station Parade, and renting out space to a bank and an estate agent. He went on to found the County Garage, which features in so many photographs of Gerrards Cross.

Industry

The only significant industry in Gerrards Cross was that of brick making. Brick and tile works were common throughout the Chilterns and there were at least three kilns near Gerrards Cross. The brick kiln on the Orchehill estate seems to have closed down before 1842. At nearby Marsham Farm, however, Henry Piner is listed from 1853 to 1869 as a brickmaker. He is described as a farmer and brickmaker in 1861 when he was employing 16 men. Next door to him, William Piner is listed as a brickmaker. In 1871, Mark Dancer, oven tile maker, and James Halsey, potter, are listed. Again, in 1881, George Alsford is shown as a tile maker, and in 1891 James Bates, with three sons, is described as an oven tile maker. The kiln is marked as the Chalfont Pottery on the 1898 Ordnance Survey map.

29　Henry Bonsey, butcher, East Common, c.1900.

Joseph Coleman, a 45-year-old brick and tile manufacturer, was living at the brick kiln, Austenwood Common, in 1881. He employed four men and a boy, some of whom lived at nearby Woodbine Cottages, a row of six houses fronting the Common. In subsequent censuses Coleman was living in Chalfont St Peter itself, but still called himself a brick and tile manufacturer. George Bunce, brick field labourer, was still living in Woodbine Cottages in 1901.

There was another old-established kiln near Stampwell Farm, Chalfont St Peter. Here, in 1851, John Swallow, born in Deptford, master potter, was employing 11 men and a boy. By 1861 Robert Swallow employed 10 men and a boy there, whereas in 1871 the number employed was down to seven men and three boys, and by 1881 to six men and a boy.

On the Oxford Road, near the *Bull Inn*, was a builder's yard run by Daniel Hunt, who employed 10 men and three boys in 1881. This may be the same yard as that later operated by Henry Cocks, builder and undertaker, which formed lot 2 in the sale of the Bulstrode estate in 1932.

Servants

The most numerous group in Gerrards Cross society were servants. As was generally the case in Victorian England, few of these would have been recruited from the local area and it appears that few stayed long in one position. Few, for instance, survive in the Gerrards Cross census records from one decade to the next. Numbers employed at the major houses show subtle changes over the period.

Col Reid rented Bulstrode from 1841-52, after which the house was let to Francis Edwards, a lawyer and financier until 1860. In the 1851 census, only Bulstrode Garden House, with a market gardener and a household of three headed by a gardener, is shown. In 1861 only three servants and no principals were listed.

Having rebuilt the house, the Duke of Somerset was present in 1871 when 25 indoor servants are listed. Household accounts survive for this period, which suggest that there were 25 indoor staff, up to 20 gardeners, nine grooms, two bricklayers, two sawyers and two carpenters.[3]

At Orchehill, William Blount and his wife Lady Charlotte kept a smaller establishment; one of them was generally in residence. In 1851 when both were present they had six indoor servants and a governess. In the lodges were a gardener and an ex-member of the Mess of Somerset House, with a coachman and a general servant in the Mews. This was fairly typical of the Blount's period at Orchehill. In 1901, when John Ashton Cross, a 55-year-old solicitor was in residence, there were nine indoor servants, a married butler in one of the lodges, a gardener, two garden boys, a coachman, groom and stable lad. By 1903, Cross had moved to Alderbourne Manor.

John Bramley-Moore of Langley Lodge was never present on census night. Nor was his successor, Colonel Le Poer Trench, who called the house St Hubert's. As a major sporting estate, however, with its own gas works, St Hubert's must have been a major employer, especially as Edward VII visited the house several times. Alderbourne, an estate on the south-east boundary of the new parish, was occupied by the Rev. Way, a relative of the Ways of Denham Place. He had eight servants in 1881 and his widow kept seven servants in 1891.

Ethorpe (previously called Fernacre Cottage) and Woodhill were very different in character to the major estates in that they had many different occupants during this period. With one exception, the principals were in residence at the time of each census. Ethorpe had at least 11 tenants, while Woodhill had at least eight. Whilst the number of servants kept at these houses was above the number gentility demanded, it was usually substantially below

Number of Servants in Large Houses						
	Bulstrode	Orchehill	Ethorpe	Woodhill	St Huberts	Alderbourne
1851	na	7	2	?	na	Ag lab only ?
1861	3★	7	4	3	na	3
1871	25	7	5	6	3★	9
1881	6★	6	5	3	3★	8
1891	6★	9	3	4	2★	8
1901	3★	9	2	2★	2★	empty

★ indicates principal not in residence

Servants in other Large Houses		
Number of Houses	2+servants**	1 servant**
3	3	3
5	4	2
6	5	2
6	6	4
6	7	6
5	11	7

**excluding farms, retailers, PH and those cases where a sinlge servant was replacing a family member e.g when a widower had a house-keeper. Excludes also those households with persons who were probably servants elsewhere.

that kept by the major mansions. Ethorpe came nearest to them when occupied from 1869 to the early 1880s by successive Army officers. Abraham Ennis Bellairs, the next occupant, seems to have experienced mixed fortunes whilst in the house. In 1891 he had kept a nurse, cook, housemaid and coachman, but by 1901 his two servants are listed as a tailor and a laundress, scarcely the titles given to servants in an affluent household. At Woodhill there was only one census, 1891, when the household included more than three servants.

By 1881, Woodbank House, later called Raylands Mead, was occupied by Fritz Oldaker. He had been born in Gerrards Cross and was described as a retired saddler. His household included only his wife and two servants. In 1891 his widow had only one servant, but by 1901, when she was aged 85, she had two grandchildren in the house, and there were four servants.

It is not clear whether any of the residents of these major houses were encouraged to live in Gerrards Cross because of the new church, and thus support the Misses Reid's claim that the building of a church would improve the area. For such evidence it is more likely that we should look for an increase in more 'middling' people. Here the best indicator is the keeping of servants, with two generally deemed necessary to maintain a 'genteel' household. A simple count of such households shows that as the century progressed a degree of gentrification was apparent and thus the endowment of the church did in this respect fulfill the claim of those who had financed it.

Overall the proportion of the population who were servants also increased. Amongst the females who gave a form of employment in 1851, the proportion was 36 per cent. With the Duke in residence in 1871 the figure was 63 per cent, a figure that was even surpassed in 1891. Amongst males the most dramatic change was an increase in the proportion occupied in gardening (13.3 per cent in 1891, with a leap to 23 per cent by 1901).

Servants as per cent of Occupied Population						
	1851	1861	1871	1881	1891	1901
Females – Domestic Servants	35.7	38.0	62.8	56.7	64.1	62.3
Males – Domestic Servants	1.3	2.4	7.7	6.0	3.4	3.4
Males – Gardeners	8.9	12.0	7.7	12.5	13.3	23.1
Males – Coachmen & Grooms	6.3	5.4	11.8	9.5	10.5	4.1

Four

The Railway

Just as Buckinghamshire's main roads were turnpiked to serve travellers from London to Bath, Oxford and Chester, so the first railway lines pushed through the county were bound for cities like Birmingham and Bristol. The London to Birmingham Railway, later known as the London and North Western Railway, was opened in 1838, its tracks skirting the east side of Buckinghamshire. The Great Western Railway's broad-gauge line to Bristol, opened as far as Maidenhead by 1838, cut across the south of the county. Whilst Uxbridge and High Wycombe were side-lined, Slough gained attention as the stopping-off point for wealthy visitors to Eton and Windsor. Genteel houses were built at Upton Park.

The GWR was slow to provide branches to the older market towns, but a short branch from the main line into Uxbridge was completed in 1856 and was of great utility to Gerrards Cross. A proposed line from Southall to Hayes, Ruislip, Chalfont, Beaconsfield, High Wycombe and Aylesbury, which would have come a lot closer to Gerrards Cross, was dropped in favour of the branch from the main line at Maidenhead to High Wycombe, which was completed in 1854. The extension of this branch to Aylesbury was further delayed until 1863. There were further plans to build lines from London direct to High Wycombe in 1875 and 1881, but both failed through lack of finance and the necessary backing of one of the big railway companies.

Neither the L&NWR nor the GWR saw any merit in building a branch to Amersham. It was left to the Metropolitan Railway to serve the centre of Buckinghamshire. Their line from Harrow to Rickmansworth opened in 1887, was extended to Chesham in 1889, and to Amersham and Aylesbury in 1892. This line gained strategic importance when the Manchester Sheffield and Lincolnshire Railway came to an agreement whereby through trains from Manchester and Sheffield could join the Metoprolitan Railway at Quainton Road, north of Aylesbury, and run through into London. By the time the link was opened in 1899, the Manchester Sheffield and Lincolnshire Railway had been renamed the Great Central Railway. Its trains used the Metropolitan line as far as Hampstead where they branched off to the new Great Central station at Marylebone.

The Great Western and Great Central Joint Railway

The working relationship between the Great Central Railway and the Metropolitan Railway proved difficult, even before the new line to Marylebone was opened. As negotiations with the Metropolitan Railway over the precise terms and costs of running Great Central trains over Metropolitan rails became increasingly heated, the Great Central Railway looked for an alternative route into London. At the same time, the Great Western Railway was anxious to improve its journey times from Paddington to Birmingham. It promoted a direct line from London to High Wycombe, from where the existing GWR branch to Princes Risborough would be up-graded and extended north to

30   Gerrards Cross Station, 1907, with the newly built shops on Packhorse Road on the left.

Bicester and Banbury. Negotiations between the Great Central and the Great Western proved far more harmonious and, in 1899, the two companies formed a Joint Committee to build the new line. Much to the annoyance of the businessmen of Uxbridge, the line was to pass north of the town on its way through Gerrards Cross and Beaconsfield towards High Wycombe. The Great Central was to make a junction from their existing line, north of Aylesbury, to join the new route near Thame.

The residents of Gerrards Cross were aware of the possibility of a railway at least as early as December 1895, when the new Parish Council passed a motion in favour of the proposed Harrow, Uxbridge & High Wycombe Railway, which was to pass through Gerrards Cross. This independent company lacked sufficient financial resources, however, and its projected line was taken over by the Metropolitan Railway. Their branch line to Uxbridge eventually opened in 1904. In December 1896, the Great Western Railway unveiled their counter proposal, which would give Gerrards Cross a station on the new

GWR main line to London. Gerrards Cross Parish Council approved the new scheme, but requested that at least one fast train, up and down, should stop at Gerrards Cross, each morning and afternoon. They also expressed concern that the planned station would be accessed from Bull Lane. With commendable foresight, they resolved that 'any station to be of use to Gerrards Cross should be so centrally situated as to meet the requirements of the present inhabitants and of the future extension of the place which is likely to result on all sides of the Common after the advent of the railway'. In April 1897, the Council received a letter from Mr Nelson, solicitor to the GWR, agreeing to place the station behind the Pilgrims' Home. Council members thanked their Chairman, Col Le Poer Trench, for his able advocacy on their behalf.

Building the Railway
The contract for building the section of railway from Northolt Junction to High Wycombe was awarded to R.W. Pauling & Co., of Westminster.

31 Gerrards Cross Station, 1908, showing the railwaymen's cottages on Packhorse Road and the new houses on Bulstrode Way on the right.

They established offices, stables and a shed for 34 locomotives at Gerrards Cross and used four steam cranes, 12 steam navvies, 715 tip wagons and 120 permanent way trucks on the project. They employed 1,500 navvies on the contract, 200-300 of whom were housed in a group of huts between Oak End Way and Station Road. The contractors had to cut a 40ft deep, one-mile-long cutting at Gerrards Cross. They had also to build bridges over the cutting for Bull Lane, Packhorse Road, Marsham Lane and Mill Lane. The other major engineering work was the construction of the two-part viaduct over Lower Road and the River Misbourne. The arches were ample enough to accommodate the dual-carriageway Chalfont St Peter by-pass in the 1960s, and the six-lane M25, completed in 1986.

At Gerrards Cross, the schoolmaster, C.E. Colston, admitted many of the navvies' children to the local school. The vicar, the Rev. J.M. Glubb, opened a mission hut and appointed James Sail as his railway missionary. The Parish Council insisted in January 1902 that covered privies be provided for the hut dwellers. The Great Western Railway built a house for the Station Master and a row of six railwaymen's cottages on Packhorse Road. Gerrards Cross Station was built in Great Western style, but it was unusual in being a two-storey structure, with the entrance from Station Approach on the first floor.

The Impact of the Railway on Gerrards Cross

The Great Western and Great Central Joint Railway opened to goods traffic on 20 November 1905 and to passengers on 2 April 1906. There was no doubt that the railway was to have a profound effect on Gerrards Cross.

Timetable, Great Western Railway, 1910

Direction	Time at GX	Stops	Destination/origin	Origin	Time to London	
up	8.04	Semi Fast	To Paddington	Aylesbury	31	
up	8.47	Semi Fast	To Paddington	Aylesbury	28	
up	8.52		To West Ealing	Gerrards Cross		
up	9.18	Semi Fast	To Paddington	Oxford	30	
up	10.06	Semi Fast	To Paddington	Oxford	29	
up	11.03	Semi Fast	To Paddington	Aylesbury	36	
up	12.53	Only Greenford	To Paddington	Oxford	27	
up	14.54	Semi Fast	To Paddington	Aylesbury	31	
up	16.01	Semi Fast	To Paddington	Oxford	29	
up	16.20		To Rusilip	Aylesbury		Saturday only
up	17.54	Semi Fast	To Paddington	Aylesbury	33	
up	18.42	All except Westbourne Park	To Paddington	Aylesbury	38	
up	20.19	All except Westbourne Park	To Paddington	High Wycombe	40	
up	22.24	All except Greenford	To Paddington	Princes Risborough	38	
down	7.32	All except Ealing Broadway	From Paddington	Oxford	37	
down	8.49	All except Westbourne Park	From Paddington	Oxford	38	
down	10.05	All except Ealing Broadway	From Paddington	Aylesbury	35	
down	12.14	Only Denham	From Paddington	Oxford	29	
down	13.57	Semi Fast	From Paddington	Aylesbury	30	
down	15.14	Semi Fast	From Paddington	Oxford	34	
down	16.35	Semi Fast	From Paddington	Aylesbury	33	
down	17.32		To Ealing Broadway	Gerrards Cross		
down	17.49	Semi Fast	From Paddington	Aylesbury	29	
down	18.54	Semi Fast	From Paddington	Oxford	30	
down	19.51	Semi Fast	From Paddington	Aylesbury	31	
own	21.41	All except Westbourne Park	From Paddington	Aylesbury	41	

Timetable, Great Central Railway, 1910

Direction	Time at GX	Stops	Destination/origin	Origin/destination	Time to London	
up	6.43	Terminates	GX	High Wycombe	na	
up	7.53	All Stations	To Marylebone	High Wycombe	40	
up	8.25	Fast	To Marylebone	High Wycombe	25	
up	9.08	Fast	To Marylebone	High Wycombe	25	
up	9.46	Rusilip Only	To Marylebone	Calvert	28	
up	11.26	All Stations	To Marylebone	Woodford & Hinton	44	
up	13.52	All except Northolt	To Marylebone	Woodford & Hinton	47	
up	14.30	All except Northolt	To Marylebone	Gerrards Cross	49	Saturday only
up	15.43	All	To Marylebone	High Wycombe	40	
up	16.20	All	To Marylebone	Aylesbury	40	Saturday only
up	17.33	All	To Marylebone	High Wycombe	40	
up	19.21	All except Northolt	To Marylebone	High Wycombe	39	
up	20.48	All except Northolt	To Marylebone	High Wycombe	40	
up	22.04	All except Northolt	To Marylebone	Calvert	40	
up	20.48	Terminates	GX	High Wycombe	na	
down	5.55	All except Northolt	From Marylebone	High Wycombe	40	
down	6.50	All except Northolt	From Marylebone	Calvert	40	
down	7.15	Semi Fast	From Marylebone	High Wycombe	35	
down	7.50	All except Northolt	From Marylebone	High Wycombe	40	
down	9.19	All	From Marylebone	Woodford & Hinton	42	
down	10.05		From Ruislip	Aylesbury		
down	12.02	All	From Marylebone	Princes Risborough	48	
down	14.12	All	From Marylebone	High Wycombe	42	except Saturday
down	14.14	All except Northolt	From Marylebone	Woodford & Hinton	39	Saturday only
down	14.35	Semi Fast	From Marylebone	High Wycombe	35	Saturday only
down	16.16	All	From Marylebone	High Wycombe	36	
down	17.18	Only Ruislip	From Marylebone	High Wycombe	28	
down	18.07	Fast	From Marylebone	Calvert	25	
down	19.06	Semi Fast	From Marylebone	High Wycombe	31	except Saturday
down	19.08	Semi Fast	From Marylebone	High Wycombe	32	Saturday only
down	20.40	All except Northolt	From Marylebone	High Wycombe	40	
down	23.00	All except Northolt	From Marylebone	High Wycombe	40	
down	0.30	All except Northolt	From Marylebone	High Wycombe	40	

32 The staff of Gerrards Cross Station in 1919.

The fields around the new station were already being surveyed for new roads and houses, and no less a figure than Sam Fay, General Manager of the Great Central Railway, had come to live at Woodbank, on Bull Lane. He had a new wing added to Woodbank, and his 18-acre estate was valued at £6,750 in 1910. As a landowner he ranked locally only after Sir John Ramsden and Colonel Le Poer Trench.

Sam Fay created the first railway company publicity department, which used the slogan 'Live in the Country' to promote the Great Central suburban trains to Beaconsfield, High Wycombe, Rickmansworth and Aylesbury. The same slogan was taken up by the promoters of the Latchmoor Estate, whose brochure reassured potential residents that Sam Fay himself lived at Gerrards Cross, thereby guaranteeing a good

rail service to London.[1] This publicity drive predates the Metropolitan Railway's 'Metroland' promotion by nearly ten years.

Separate main line services were run by the Great Western Railway into Paddington and the Great Central Railway into Marylebone. In 1910, the GWR service comprised 12 London-bound trains each weekday, the fastest service, the 8.47 to Paddington, taking 28 minutes, including stops at Denham and Ruislip. The majority of trains to Paddington were semi-fast and took 30 minutes. The Great Central Railway provided 11 trains to London, the fastest services, the 8.25 and 9.08 to Marylebone taking 25 minutes non-stop. Evidently no early arrival in an office was required, as the earliest train to Marylebone arrived at 8.33. The majority of trains to

Marylebone took 40 minutes because they stopped at all stations. In the evening, the non-stop service from Marylebone to Gerrards Cross left at 18.07 and took 25 minutes. The last service from Marylebone left at 30 minutes after midnight. In 1910, the return fare from Gerrards Cross to Paddington or Marylebone was 4s. first class, and 2s. third class, whilst season tickets were £20 and £12 4s. respectively.

The Uxbridge Branch

The Great Western Railway built a short branch to Uxbridge, diverting from the main line at Denham and running into a new terminus at High Street, Uxbridge. This station was not opened until 1 May 1907. Although its main purpose was to give the people of Uxbridge access to the new main line, some in Gerrards Cross saw this as an opportunity to preserve the established link with their local market town and pressed for a through service to Uxbridge. Not everyone was in favour: a correspondent to the *Slough, Windsor & Eton Express* pointed out that 'if Gerrards Cross is to become a prosperous town, it will be necessary for all the inhabitants to spend as much money in it as possible. The expenditure of Gerrards Cross cash at Uxbridge is not likely to be beneficial to Gerrards Cross, and residents of the latter place will do well to bear this in mind if they are asked to sign a petition to the G.W.R. Company for a motor bus service between Gerrards Cross and Uxbridge'.[2]

33 The Great Central Railway Company advertisement for train services on the new line, April 1906.

In the event the GWR did provide 'motor buses', that is, steam-powered railcars, which traversed the branch and ran through to Gerrards Cross, taking 15 minutes for the full journey. The service was operated with one railcar arriving at Gerrards Cross early in the morning and going backwards and forwards to Uxbridge all day. This preserved Gerrards Cross's link with its nearest market town and provided transport for servants, shopworkers and school children, as well as customers visiting the larger shops in Uxbridge. The service was maintained until the outbreak of war in 1939. Passenger services on the branch were not reintroduced after the war and goods traffic to Uxbridge High Street ended in 1962.[3]

Timetable, Gerrards Cross to Uxbridge, 1925												
	am	am	am	am	am	pm	pm	pm	pm	pm	pm	pm
Gerrards Cross	6 44	8 08	9 08	10 18	11 25	1 12	2 23	4 21	5 49	7 00	8 39	10 20
Denham	6 51	8 15	9 15	10 25	11 32	1 19	2 30	4 29	5 57	7 07	8 46	10 27
Uxbridge	6 59	8 24	9 21	10 34	11 41	1 28	2 36	4 38	6 06	7 16	8 55	10 36
Uxbridge	7 05	8 37	9 25	10 50	12 17	1 39	2 45	5 22	6 38	7 30	9 20	10 50
Denham	7 11	8 43	9 33	10 56	12 23	1 45	2 51	5 28	6 44	7 36	9 26	10 56
Gerrards Cross	7 18	8 50	9 40	11 03	12 30	1 52	2 58	5 35	6 51	7 43	9 33	11 03

Five

Shops and Offices

As the Great Western & Great Central Joint Railway was nearing completion, the new owners of the Orchehill estate, James and William Gurney, were planning to develop the land north of the railway. They employed the surveyor, Legender Myers, of Messrs Kerkham, Burgess & Myers, to lay out new roads. His surviving drawings show that he earmarked a distinct plot of land for 'shop plots 50ft fronts and 120ft deep'. This land was bounded on the west by Packhorse Road, on the north by a footpath which was to become Oak End Way, on the east by Marsham Lane and on the south by the railway. Another new road, later to become Station Road, ran east to west, dividing the new commercial area in two. By 1910-12, this block of commercial land was divided amongst 28 different owners, although only a small part had been developed. The best plots proved to be those with a frontage on Packhorse Road. In 1912, the site on the corner of Oak End Way was valued at £5,926 per acre, compared with £2,500-£2,700 for nearby sites in Oak End Way and Station Road. The lowest values away from Packhorse Road were about £1,500 per acre.

Station Road

The first commercial development began in May 1906 when J.C. Richards & Co., who had set up a branch builder's yard in Station Road, began to build a row of four shops near the junction of Station Road with Packhorse Lane. These shops were designed by the local architects, Kerkham, Burgess & Myers, and were initially occupied by F.C. Moss, baker, Leonard Tayler, grocer, Charles Berry, watchmaker, and A. Woodbridge, ironmonger. In July 1906, Y.J. Lovell & Son began to build a cottage and office in the builder's yard they had recently set up on the corner of Station Road and Marsham Lane.[1] Lovell's premises were to extend further up the south side of Station Road and later expanded to the opposite side of the road. The present office block on the corner of Marsham Lane was built by Lovells in 1969. Another local builder, Ernest Burgess, also set up his yard on the south side of Station Road.

In January 1907, William Payne, a bicycle maker who lived at St Hubert's Cottages, East Common, commissioned Kerkham, Burgess & Myers to design a row of three shops on Packhorse Road, between Station Road and the railway bridge. These were to be occupied by Barclays Bank, William Payne's cycle shop, and William Weston, estate agent. In March 1907, Henry Bonsey, who had a butcher's shop on East Common, commissioned Kerkham, Burgess & Myers to design two shops opposite F.C. Moss's bakery. One of the new shops was taken by his son, Frederick Bonsey, also a butcher, and the other was let to Richard Exton, grocer. In 1909, William Weston put up a temporary public hall in Station Road, but this was later converted into a garage by J. Bailey & Co.

To the south side of the railway line, Hampton & Sons were laying out Bulstrode Way

34 Station Road, *c.*1908. The four shops on the left side were designed by Kerkham, Burgess & Myers for J.C. Richards & Co., whose builder's yard was further down the street. One of the shops was occupied by Austin Woodbridge. On the other side of the road are two unusual shops, also designed by Kerkham, Burgess & Myers, in 1907, for Henry Bonsey.

35 Leonard Harry Tayler's grocery store, 3 Station Road, *c.*1910. L.H. Tayler was for many years a member of Gerrards Cross Parish Council.

36 Austin Woodbridge's hardware shop, Station Road, 1908. These premises were known as London House and were later occupied by S. Field & Co. and then by Lord Brothers, also ironmongers.

37 One of Henry Bonsey's new shops on Station Road was occupied by his son, Frederick H. Bonsey, in 1908.

and Marsham Way for residential development. The frontage to Packhorse Road, between the railway bridge and Marsham Lane, was, however, suitable for commercial development. The postmaster, Arthur Matthews, purchased the plot of land on the corner of Packhorse Road and Marsham Way and, in August 1907, applied for building regulation consent to build a new sub-Post Office there, to replace the existing premises opposite the *Bull Hotel*.[2] He continued to combine his trade as a tailor with his role of postmaster until the building of a main Post Office put him out of business in 1913. His premises, numbered 29 Station Parade, were taken over by Sidney Bates, tailor, and later occupied by A.J. Hall & Co., tailors.

Station Parade

Meanwhile Henry Brown, a builder from Stoke Newington who was developing the North Park Estate at Gerrards Cross, had purchased much of the land fronting Packhorse Road, between Oak End Way and Station Road. In September 1907, he applied for permission to build six shops there.[3] These shops, with

flats above, were designed by Kerkham, Burgess & Myers in the 'tudorbethan' style then becoming popular in suburbs around London. The shops were numbered 1-6 Station Parade and the first occupants were Wood & Son, confectioners; Walter Poole, fruiterer; Sarah Heath, draper; the London & County Bank; Rayner & Son, chemists; and Cecil Cox, stationer. At the same time, Legender Myers himself applied for permission to build an office next to these shops. This was called Orchehill Chambers, and was to accommodate offices for the architects, Kerkham, Burgess & Myers. When this partnership was dissolved, Burgess and Myers moved to their offices in Burkes Parade, Beaconsfield, whilst their assistant, Edgar Ranger, continued at Orchehill Chambers. Y.J. Lovell & Son later had their drawing office here, with Bill Scales in charge. In October 1907, The London & South Western Bank applied for permission to develop the plot on the corner of Packhorse Road and Station Road, next to William Payne's shops. This banking chain was later absorbed by Barclays and the premises were then occupied by Howard Roberts, grocers. By

38 Richard Exton's grocery store, Station Road, 1908. This shop was later taken over by Vernon Brown & Co., corn merchants.

39 Shops in Station Parade, Packhorse Road, designed by Kerkham, Burgess & Myers, 1907, for William Payne. In the centre is William Payne's cycle shop, flanked by Barclays Bank and William Weston, estate agent.

40 One of the first buildings on the other side of the railway bridge was a sub-Post Office and tailor's shop, built in 1907 for Arthur Matthews.

41 1-6 Station Parade, Gerrards Cross, for sale by auction, 11 May 1910.

42 Wood & Son, confectioner, Station Parade, 1908.

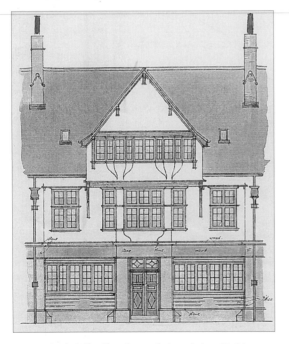

43 Orchehill Chambers, designed by Kerkham, Burgess & Myers, 1907.

the close of 1907, there were shops fronting Packhorse Road all the way from Oak End Way to Marsham Way and these soon became known as 'Station Parade'.

Oak End Way

In December 1907, another locally based architect, Percy Hopkins, who was developing the Milton Park estate, Bull Lane, applied for permission to erect six shops halfway down Oak End Way. These shops followed the now established pattern for Gerrards Cross in having half-timbered façades, but they were not as elegant or well-built as those in Station Parade.[4] Percy Hopkins occupied one of the units himself and let the remainder to Charles Springell, hairdresser; Ellen Ives, boot maker; Mrs Stevens; S.W. Golding; and Alfred Martin, butcher. Percy Hopkins also developed the shops near the corner of Oak End Way and Station Parade, one of which was taken by

International Stores. In 1913, he built the Oak End Hall and Assembly Rooms, where there was a hall 50ft by 25ft seating 250 people and with a sprung floor for dancing. In 1917 and in 1921, dancing classes were on offer at the Assembly Rooms on Saturday mornings from the Misses Bostock and Willoughby Brown, who travelled down from Emperor's Gate, London. In the afternoon, Madame Paripa Rosa Sherwood, of Belsize Road, South Hampstead, offered classes for children and adults.

Percy Hopkins also built the row of eight cottages on the corner of Oak End Way and Marsham Lane, and designed the dairy on the corner of Oak End Way and South Park. Despite the efforts of Percy Hopkins and his Oak End Estate Ltd, Oak End Way remained a secondary commercial area.

The vacant plot in Station Parade, next to Orchehill Chambers, remained vacant until 1910, when a shop and house were built for

44   Station Parade, Gerrards Cross, *c.*1940, with Orchehill Chambers in the centre and, in the distance, the new premises of Barclays Bank, built 1911-12.

45 In 1907, Percy Hopkins designed two small shops in Oak End Way for Herbert George Trace, one of the promoters of the Milton Park estate. One of them was occupied by A. Smith, dairyman, in 1908.

46 The other small shop on Oak End Way was occupied in 1908 by Thomas Henry Roff, fruiterer and greengrocer.

47 This block of six shops was promoted in 1908 by Percy Hopkins, who occupied one of the units himself.

P.B. Spaull of Ealing, stationer. The corner plot at the junction of Station Road was filled by new premises for the London, County and Westminster Bank, designed by Cheston & Parkins in 1912. The commercial centre was to be extended northwards into Packhorse Road in 1912 with the completion of new premises for Barclays Bank. They brought in the Windsor architects, Edgington & Spink, to design the bank, but Y.J. Lovell & Son got the building contract.[5] This was the third prestigious bank building, a sign that the financial community had confidence in the further growth of Gerrards Cross and its ability to attract wealthy residents. By 1915, the only places in Buckinghamshire with more banks were the major towns of Aylesbury, High Wycombe and Slough. Gerrards Cross and

48   The turning into Oak End Way was dominated by the Park Creamery, a remarkable thatched house, built in 1909 to the design of Walker & Hopkins.

49   By 1912, Gerrards Cross had expanded sufficiently to warrant a main Post Office. It was built for the Postmaster General to the designs of Kemp & How.

50 In 1913, the gap between the sub-Post Office and the railway bridge was filled by a row of seven shops promoted by George Francis Duck, estate agent, and built by Claude Baldwin. Opposite were the GWR cottages built in 1905.

Beaconsfield ranked equally, but both were ahead of Amersham, even with its new suburb of Amersham on the Hill.

In 1912, a new main Post Office, designed by Kemp & How, was built on the corner of Marsham Way.[6] The Postmaster General evidently shared the banks' confidence in Gerrards Cross. The only significant gap on Station Parade was filled in 1913 when the builder-surveyor partnership of Baldwin & Duck built the row of seven shops between Marsham Way and the railway bridge.[7] They were originally numbered 21-17 Station Parade, and were first occupied by William Perkins, draper; Sidney Bates, furnisher; William Matthews, bootmaker; Charles Palmer,

grocer; Albert Bumstead, greengrocer; George Newman, baker; and F. Batte, fishmonger.

With the Great War and the lack of resources in its immediate aftermath, commercial development did not resume until the 1920s. In 1922, a new Congregational Church was built beyond the Post Office on Packhorse Road, and William Payne built two shops on the corner of Packhorse Road and Bulstrode Way. Until this time, the shops in Gerrards Cross were operated mostly by independent traders, whose advertisements stressed personal service. G.A. Sage, grocer, newly arrived at 24 Station Parade in 1917, claimed to roast coffee daily on the premises and to blend tea to suit the water of the district.

51 The sale of the Ethorpe estate in 1923 made it possible to develop the west side of Packhorse Road. The new shops called The Highway were designed by J. Stanley Beard in 1925.

The Highway

The multiple shops began to move into Gerrards Cross in the mid-1920s with the building of The Highway, a row of 13 shops built on land released by the sale of the Ethorpe estate in 1923. The project began that year with a proposal from the local baker and confectioner, George Newman, and the cinema architect and resident of Gerrards Cross, J. Stanley Beard, to build a row of three shops with a cinema, dance hall and café behind. Their 1923 plans for the 'Picture Playhouse', on the corner of Ethorpe Crescent, were scaled down in 1925 to produce the present buildings.[8] In 1929, The Playhouse boasted a seating capacity of 567 and an orchestra of eight first-class musicians. By 1931, it claimed to be the 'Theatre De Luxe of the District [with] the most life-like reproduction of all the best and biggest talking

films immediately on general release dates'. Private boxes to seat four were available at 12s. 6d.

Early occupants of the shops in The Highway were W.H. Smith & Sons, newsagents; George Newman himself; and J.W. Sturgess, tailor. J. Stanley Beard also designed a further 10 shops, extending from Ethorpe Crescent to the *Ethorpe Hotel*, which were built between 1924 and 1926. This block included a new Midland Bank; Gapps grocery stores (one of a chain specialising in tea); J.E. Stutter, watchmaker; Benard Kemmler, music stores; Waitrose grocery stores; Achille Serre & Co, cleaners; Coopers, fishmongers; International Stores, moving from Oak End Way; and the National Provincial Bank. Two of the independent traders soon moved out, the watchmaker giving way to Boots the Chemists, which opened in 1932,

52 The new shops called The Highway included branches of W.H. Smith and Boots the Chemist.

53 The shopping complex called The Highway included the Playhouse Cinema, also designed by J. Stanley Beard in 1925.

and the music dealer being replaced by an extension to Waitrose.[9]

The Shopkeepers
With hindsight, it is clear that the shops were going to be very successful but, from the standpoint of the original shopkeepers, there was nothing inevitable about this process. It was only the collective enterprise of the traders that caused the shopping centre to achieve critical mass. The editor of the 1935 directory, admittedly a local trader himself, talked up the local shops:

> On population figures, approximately 3,300, could be classified as a village, but the shops are not village shops. Is it surprising that newcomers are getting into the habit of calling it a town? Adequate stocks, good variety, keen prices, attractive display and modern lighting. Every trade is represented and apart from five or six 'multiple shops' that have arrived in recent years, a very stimulating feature is the number of enterprising individual shopkeepers.

Overall the number of shops rose from 29 in 1911 to 59 in 1940, with most of this growth occurring before 1929.

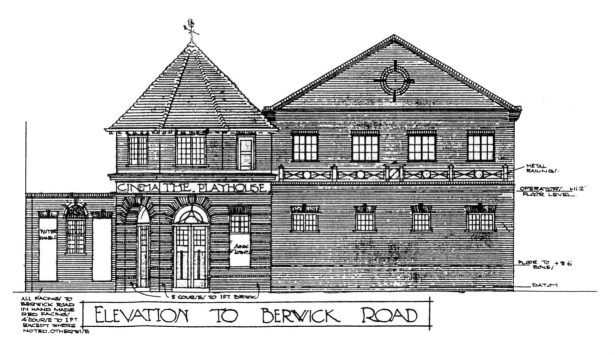

Traders in Gerrards Cross, 1911–1940					
	1911	1917	1929	1935	1940
Food (General)	6	8	14	15	16
Baker	2	2	2	3	4
Butcher	3	2	3	3	3
Confectioner	2	3	4	5	4
Newsagent	1		3	2	2
Furnisher	2	2	1	1	1
Home Ware	2	2	2	2	2
Clothing	3	13	14	9	13
Shoes	3	2	3	4	3
Chemist	2	2	2	3	3
Other Shop	2	1	2	4	3
Dry Cleaner	1	2	4	5	5
	29	39	54	56	59

Only a few of the shopkeepers, like Bonsey, Payne and Wood, were local to the area. The process whereby others decided that Gerrards Cross was a good place from which to trade is obscure, but some, like H.G. Wells' Mr Polly, may have spent their weekends touring the outer London suburbs looking for a place to set up business. Jack Cohen followed the same course in the 1930s although he found no suitable site in the area. A number of independent traders moved from West London, notably P.B. Spaull, who sold a flourishing stationery business in Ealing to move to Station Parade. Others established a second branch in Gerrards Cross whilst retaining their original business, such as Bolton & Son, house furnishers, whose main shop was in Brentford. S.J. Muir, photographer and frame maker, also operated in West Ealing. From Uxbridge came Rayner & Son, pharmacists, and Vernon Brown, corn and seedsman. John Harding & Sons, holders of the Royal Warrant as butchers, had branches in Slough and Farnham Common. The proximity of the expanding settlements of Amersham and Beaconsfield afforded the opportunity for some to trade there as well as at Gerrards Cross. Amongst the newcomers, Sidney Bates deserves special mention. In 1921 he was operating from two units, one a furnishers at the far end of Station Parade, south of the railway, and the other at the north end of Station Parade as an antique furnisher.

The Multiples

The first multiple to arrive in Gerrards Cross was International Stores, who had 11 grocery shops in Buckinghamshire and opened their shop in Oak End Way before 1915. They later moved to The Highway. A more specialist multiple was Stowell's, the wine importers, with a head office in Ealing.

Waitrose's Gerrards Cross branch was open from 1928 to 1969 and in the early days it was one of their flagship shops, soon expanding into what had been a music shop next door. Its advertising highlighted 'the choicest goods in many cases with prices cheaper than those of the London stores'. The chain was particularly keen to promote its delivery service which was available in all stores. The Gerrards Cross shop covered a wider geographical area than most Waitrose shops and, therefore, provided motor vans to deliver the goods as well as the usual bicycle deliveries. The fleet of vans offered five regular deliveries daily within Gerrards Cross, to the Chalfonts, Seer Green, Jordans, Stoke Poges and Slough, and a daily service to all places within a ten-mile radius. They also offered a telephone ordering service whereby customers could ring up each day, two or three times a week, and place orders which would be despatched the same day. In addition customers could arrange for Waitrose telephone orders department to ring them at a pre-arranged time each day to take their order.

54 Station Road about 1950, when most of the former builders yards were occupied by offices and flats.

Sainsbury's did not open their store at Gerrards Cross until 1932. They took over the premises at 8 Station Parade, formerly occupied by P.B. Spaull, stationer.[10]

Cleaners

A trade which was one of the few exceptions to local personal service was laundry and cleaning services. Of the five firms listed as dyers and cleaners in Buckinghamshire in 1915, two had premises in Gerrards Cross. John Jackson was listed as a 'cleaner and dyer', but also ran an agency for the Royal Bucks Laundry, Chesham.

Another early arrival was Eastman & Son, a London firm of dyers and cleaners which had five branches in Buckinghamshire, including Gerrards Cross and Beaconsfield. The number of advertisements for laundries in the local directory after 1918 suggests that the upper middle class, needing clean linen but faced with a shortage of servants, were not averse to sending material into commercial hands.

Garages

By the 1920s, all the new houses in Gerrards Cross were built with garages and most owners

55 The shops on the left, adjoining the *Packhorse Inn*, were built in the 1950s, where Hunstan's Hall, with its 1796 datestone, had once stood.

of older properties had built garages in their gardens. There was therefore a very strong demand for motor cars in Gerrards Cross, initially met by J. Bailey who extended his garage at the corner of Pinewood Close in 1911. In about 1920, Bailey & Co. moved to premises in Station Road which had formerly been a public hall. There were constant complaints to the Parish Council about pipes from Bailey's petrol pumps obstructing the footpath there. The firm later changed its name to Gerrards Cross Car Services Ltd, and built elegant showrooms with flats above on the south side of Station Road. This building, erected in 1933, is now called Marsham Chambers, 16 Station Road.[11] The garage continued after the war as Lewis's Garage.

William Payne had turned his cycle shop in Station Parade into the County Garage by 1917. This was taken over by Norman Daintree who further extended the premises in 1926, 1931 and 1933. The County Garage was later purchased by E.L. Colston of St Bernards, Oak End Way. The Oxford Road Garage was run by G.R. Taylor, who extended the buildings there in 1931. This garage was on the site of Claude Baldwin's builders yard, which in turn had been built on the site of the old smithy, opposite the *Bull Inn*. Gordon White & Co., motor engineers, of Chalfont St Peter, built a new garage beyond the Congregational Church in 1933. This was the first garage to have a proper forecourt for the petrol pumps.

One of the more unusual building regulations applications was the proposal in 1937 to connect both halves of Station Parade by building a row of shops over the railway. The scheme resembled the ill-fated Tesco scheme of 2005, but in this

56 The Station Master's house and six railwaymen's cottages, built in 1905 between Bulstrode Way and the railway bridge, were replaced in about 1960 by a new Lloyds Bank and a row of 10 shops.

case the shops were to be supported on steel beams. Eton Rural District Council turned down the application.[12]

The next opportunity for commercial development came in about 1960 with the demolition of the railway cottages which stood on Packhorse Road, between Bulstrode Way and the railway bridge. These were replaced by a row of shops including a new Lloyds Bank. The land north of the *Packhorse Inn* was also developed at this time with the building of two more blocks of shops, including a showroom for Southern Electricity and a branch of F.W. Woolworth. In the late 1960s and 1970s, Tesco operated a branch at the southern end of Packhorse Road in what had formerly been the Wycombe Superstore, but this was only a small self-service shop.

In the 1980s, a further block of shops was built on Packhorse Road, involving the relocation of the Congregational Church.

Six

Building the Houses

In 1903, whilst the railway contractors were still laying the tracks through Gerrards Cross, a local builder, Albert Fowler, was laying out a new road off Bull Lane, immediately south of the railway cutting.[1] The six terraced houses he built there were called South View and were probably the first houses to be built in Gerrards Cross as a result of the coming of the railway.

By the time the Great Western & Great Central Joint Railway opened in April 1906, Gerrards Cross was already a hive of activity. Landowners and estate agents were doing deals, architects were setting up local offices, and builders were delivering materials to their newly fenced yards. The largest single transaction was the sale in 1905 of the 193-acre Orchehill estate by Oscar Blount to the local estate agents, James and William Gurney, for £29,000.[2] The land was therefore valued at £150 per acre, at a time when agricultural land was selling at £20 per acre.

Building Regulations Plans

Before any building work could commence, applications had to be made to Amersham and Eton Rural District Councils, who had to ensure that building regulations were met, that roads were properly constructed and that the proposed sewers would be fit for the purpose. There were 12 building regulations applications to Amersham RDC in 1906 for sites in Chalfont St Peter, near Austenwood Common, as compared with 30 applications to

Eton RDC for new houses and shops within Gerrards Cross parish.

The building plan registers can be used to show the sequence of developers' proposals. The Eton R.D.C. registers show the peak number of houses proposed in Gerrards Cross during the period 1900-1940 was 55, in 1908.[3] The Amersham RDC registers provide less detail, so it is difficult to be precise as to which Chalfont St Peter plans actually relate to the Gerrards Cross area. Of those plans that can be identified as being within the Gerrards Cross area, the peak during the period 1900-1920 was 1909. In both areas 60 per cent of proposals in the latter period were made before 1911.

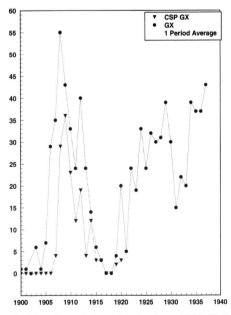

Building Regulations Applications, 1900-1940.

The sequence of actual development can be traced from the Lloyd George Valuation Survey of 1910-12 and from local street directories. The basic figures show that the pre-First World War era was the period of most sustained development, followed by the 1920s, and especially the last years of that decade. In the 1930s it was only with the opening up of the Dukes Wood and Camp Road estates, also towards the end of the decade, that rates of development matched those of the early years.

House Building in Gerrards Cross 1911-40			
	No. of Houses	No. in period	No. per year
1911*	290	290	41
1915	479	189	47
1917	479	0	0
1921	497	18	5
1929	742	245	31
1931	839	97	49
1933	879	40	20
1935	920	41	21
1938	982	62	21
1940	1107	125	42
* from 1906			

The Orchehill Estate

The Gurneys employed Legender W. Myers, a partner in the local firm of architects, Kerkham, Burgess & Myers, to divide the land around Orchehill House into 177 building plots, east and west of Packhorse Road. Opposite the house, 15 large plots were set out on Packhorse Road. Two new roads, called North Park and South Park, either side of Orchehill House, gave access to 29 very large house plots, with views over Chalfont Park. Another 32 large plots were laid out in a new road called Oval Way, either side of an ornamental spinney. Kingsway and Austenway, north of Austenwood Common, comprised 60 smaller plots. New roads called Pottery Road (later to be called Oak End Way) and the Woodlands were mapped out but no building plots had been decided upon. The area to the west of Oval Way which was to become the Latchmoor estate was earmarked for future development. The London surveyors

Robinson & Roods were also involved in the arrangements for the division and sale of the Orchehill estate.[4]

The first auction of the Orchehill building plots was held at the *Bull Inn*, Gerrards Cross, on 30 January 1906. This included plots 50-112 either side of the new roads called Kingsway and Austenway. The newspaper advertisements claimed that Gerrards Cross was one of the healthiest spots in the Home Counties and was deservedly known as 'The Brighton of Bucks'. These plots had been 'laid out for the erection of villas and country cottages, for which there is an enormous demand in the district'.[5] A sale of a further 50 lots was held at the *Bull Inn* on 5 April. A third sale, scheduled for 19 April, was cancelled as all the remaining plots had been sold by private treaty. The auctions were conducted by Messrs Curtis & Henson, of 5 Mount Street, London W.

A significant purchaser at the auction was the Circle Land Company, a development firm which operated from the same London address as the surveyors, Robinson & Roods. Another large purchaser was Charles Raffety, a High Wycombe estate agent, who bought several plots in Oval Way. Franklyn & Fisk, builders of Rickmansworth, bought several plots on Packhorse Road opposite Orchehill House. The solicitors acting for the Gurney family were Messrs Francis & How, of Chesham. Each conveyance imposed very specific conditions on purchasers and their successors, dictating building lines and the value of the houses to be built on each plot.

Kingsway and Austenway

James and William Gurney submitted plans of new roads on the Orchehill estate to Eton RDC in May 1906 and to Amersham RDC in July. Gurney family tradition has it that a section of road over Austenwood Common was constructed at dead of night so as to be a *fait accompli* the next morning. In November,

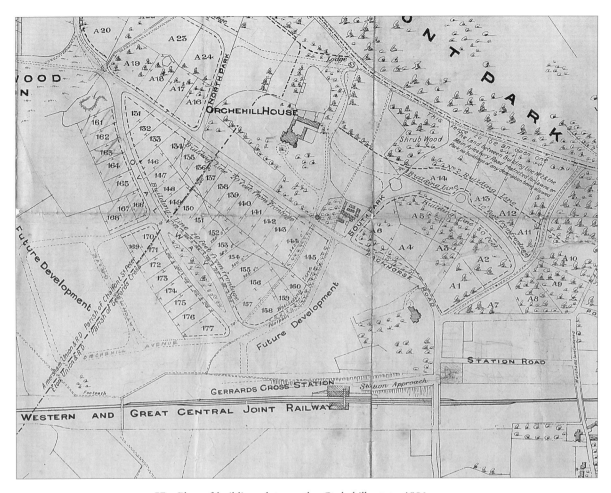

57 Plan of building plots on the Orchehill estate, 1906.

Amersham councillors formed a special sub-committee to inspect the new roads on the Orchehill estate. They decided to adopt Kingsway on condition that any damage to the surface of the road caused by builders' carts should be repaired to the satisfaction of the Council's surveyor.[6] The first two applications for building regulations approval were made to Amersham RDC by Kerkham, Burgess & Myers in February 1906. The road was not specified, but the same firm made a similar application for a house in Kingsway in April 1906. The Circle Land Company built many of the houses on Austenway and Kingsway, some for sale from £675, and some for rent, from

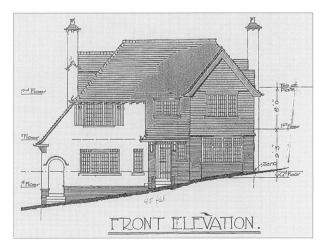

58 Badsey Cottage, Kingsway, built by the Circle Land Company, 1913.

59 The Orchehill estate did not include the *Three Pigeons*, Austenwood Common, but this was rebuilt to match the new houses by H. & C. Simonds Ltd in the 1930s.

£45 per year. Badsey Cottage, 5 Kingsway, is typical of their houses.[7]

Packhorse Road

The 1906 plan of building plots on the Orchehill estate has the east side of Packhorse Road divided into large building plots at North Park and South Park, with the grounds of Orchehill House sandwiched in the middle. On the west side, 15 medium-sized building plots extend along Packhorse Road from the proposed Orchehill Avenue to Austenwood

60 Packhorse Road, *c.*1910. The Turret House, built by Franklin & Fisk of Rickmansworth, appears on the left.

Common. These were soon snapped up by speculative builders like Franklin & Fisk of Rickmansworth, who built six houses between 1907 and 1909, including The Turrett House, St Budeaux, Selwyn, Wayside and Belmont. The land between Orchehill Avenue and Ethorpe was not developed until the sale of the Ethorpe estate in 1923.

Oval Way

Oval Way was laid out on part of the Orchehill estate by the surveyor, Legender Myers, of Kerkham Burgess & Myers. The road divides around an ornamental spinney and crosses the parish boundary into Chalfont St Peter. The building plots 150-7 and 171-7 were purchased at the 1906 sale of the Orchehill estate by Hamnett, Raffety & Co., who employed the leading London architects, Forbes & Tate, to design three of their houses. Harold Raffety himself lived at The Pollards, 3 Oval Way, on the corner of Orchehill Avenue. This house, built in 1907, is the most extravagant of the Forbes & Tate designs in Gerrards Cross, with its characteristic 'eye-brow' dormers.[8] Brown Cottage, 15 Oval Way, also built in 1907, has the same feature. Kimberley, 22 Oval Way, followed in 1908. Here Forbes & Tate evoked the style of an old corn mill, with the overhanging roof to the central gable.

The other significant architect in Oval Way is Charles Davis. He designed Woolton House, 4 Oval Way, and Glendruid, 10 Oval Way, for G. Welch in 1911, and Fencourt, 6 Oval Way, for the same client in 1913. All Saints Church, Oval Way, was built in 1912. The architect, Temple Moore, designed a large church with side aisles and a tower. Only the north aisle was in fact built.

61 Lyncroft, a large house on the west side of Packhorse Road, was designed by L.W.S. Goodbody in 1906. It later became a nursing home and was demolished c.1987.

62 Oval Way, c.1939.

63 Hillsborough Lodge, 2 Oval Way, designed by Robinson & Roods, 1909.

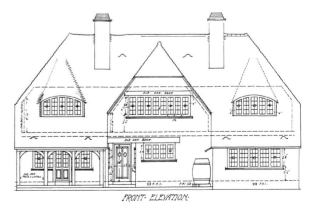

64 Brown Cottage, 15 Oval Way, designed by Forbes & Tate, 1907.

65   Stokel, 25 Oval Way.

North Park

At the sale of the Orchehill estate in 1906, many of the large building plots north of Orchehill House were purchased by Henry Brown, builder, of 329 Harrow Road, London W. His North Park estate featured in H.C. Moore's *Gerrards Cross, Beaconsfield and the Chilterns*, published in 1910:

> Situate on high ground and with beautiful surroundings, and commanding magnificent views of the celebrated Chalfont Park with its wooded slopes, and the well-known Misbourne Valley, this estate is well worth a visit from those who are seeking a residence in this locality. It is within 10 minutes walk of the station, post office, and shops, and adjoins Austen Wood Common ... The soil is gravel, and the air particularly bracing. Electric light and gas mains are on the estate, and good and pure water supply is obtained from the Rickmansworth Water Co ... Well-designed detached country houses of sound construction, and with every comfort, are being erected on sites of about half an acre at prices from £1,400 upwards freehold.

The houses on North Park appear to have been designed by Henry Brown himself and feature very heavy timber framing, particularly on the gables. His prices put him at the top of the range for builders in Gerrards Cross. Henry Brown also bought land in the commercial area and developed the fine row of six shops in Station Parade.

South Park

At the sale of the Orchehill estate in 1906, the parkland south of Orchehill House, bounded by Packhorse Road, Oak End Way and Lower Road, was laid out in 14 very large building plots. The roads called South Park, and South Park Crescent are shown. South Park Drive is drawn with dotted lines and initially follows the route of the driveway from the lodge on the Aylesbury Road to Orchehill House.

One of the first houses in South Park was Stonycroft, later known as Grit Howe, built for Harold Moreland in 1907. It was designed by the London architect, C.C. Makins, and built

66   Riva, 54 North Park, built by Henry Brown & Co., *c.*1908.

by Y.J. Lovell & Son. The garden was large enough to warrant a separate gardener's cottage. Moreland was a parish councillor from 1913 and was elected Chairman of the Council in 1920.

In 1908, John Graham Johnson designed South Park House, 8 South Park Drive, for Clement W. Windover. It too was built by Y.J. Lovell and had a gardener's cottage. Johnson & Boddy

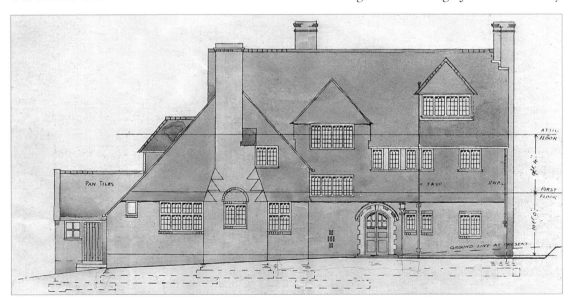

67   Grit Howe, 22, South Park Crescent, designed by C.C. Makins for Harold Moreland, 1907.

68   South Park House, 8 South Park Drive, designed by John Graham Johnson for W. Clement Windover, 1908, featured in *Modern Building Record* in 1911.

designed Noris (now Lynbury), 14 South Park Crescent, for Y.J. Lovell & Son in 1909. This house appeared in Lovell's advert in *Where to Live Round London*, 1910. (See p.143.)

The most notable house in South Park is The Tudors, originally built in 1921 for Harold William Sanderson, a director of Wallpaper Manufacturers Ltd. It was designed by the celebrated Arts and Crafts architect, Baillie Scott, and built by Jordans Village Industries, Beaconsfield. The Tudors is reputed to have cost £30,000 to build. It was later the home of Austin Reed, the men's outfitter, who opened his shop in Regent Street in 1926.

Marsham Lane

Marsham Lane was an old road running from Marsham Lodge, on Gerrards Cross Common, past Marsham Farm, towards an old brick and tile works on Lower Road called Chalfont Pottery. Several larger houses were built on

Marsham Lane. Belma, now greatly enlarged and known as Ben More, was designed in 1914 by Burgess & Myers for C.P. Lovell, then the principal partner in Y.J. Lovell & Son.[9] Dorchester House was designed by Francis W. Ferris in 1913 for Y.J. Lovell & Son. Cooldara, later to be known as Swarthmore, was designed by Bunney & Makins in 1910 for Mrs Stevenson. At the far end of the road was the extravagant Thatched House, designed in 1908 by A. Jessop Hardwick FRIBA for T.D. McMeekin.[10] It was later called Glendales but the site has since been redeveloped.

The Woodlands

The Woodlands was a new road laid out by the surveyors Robinson & Roods for their Circle Land Company. The land was purchased from James and William Gurney in August 1906. The plots were designed for large houses like Davan House, 38 The Woodlands, built

69 The Dormers, 13 South Park Crescent, designed by John Myers, 1912.

70 The Tudors, 19 South Park Crescent, designed by Baillie Scott for Harold William Sanderson, in 1920.

by Robinson & Roods in 1907 for Mrs Ada Kuhlenthal, who moved here from West Ealing. Another prominent resident was W. Haldane Porter, of Quenby, 9 The Woodlands, which was built in 1906. He was Vice Chairman and later Chairman of Gerrards Cross Parish Council. The site of Quenby has since been redeveloped. The most notable house in the Woodlands is Chiltern House, 21 The Woodlands, built for E.G. Eardley-Wilmot

in 1907. The architect, Arnold Mitchell, of 12 Hanover Square, London W., designed a very similar chalet-style house at Sonning, in Berkshire.

The Firs Estate

The Firs estate was built on the site of a former gravel pit and brick works at the south-east end of Austenwood Common. There was already a house fronting the

72   Swarthmore, Marsham Lane, c.1950. The house is now a residential home.

71   Belma, now known as Ben More, 5 Oak End Way, designed by Burgess & Myers, 1914.

73   The Thatched House, Marsham Lane, designed by A. Jessop Hardwick in 1908.

74 Davan House, 38 The Woodlands, built in 1907 by Robinson & Roods for Mrs Ada Kuhlenthal.

common called The Firs, and a row of six houses called Woodbine Cottages, built about 1880, occupied by brick and tile makers. The first section of the Firs estate was auctioned by William Weston on 11 June 1907 and comprised 55 building plots on the west side of The Queensway, Mayfield Avenue and the south side of Acrefield Road. The sale also included The Firs, two other building plots on Southside, and a gravel pit. The Firs Estate Extension was auctioned in 1908, when plots 61–109, including both sides of The Greenway, were offered. The plan showed that 11 houses had already been built on the land sold in 1907. The developers were John Bullard Harris, a former insurance agent in London, who came to live at Heatherview, Southside, about 1907, and George Burgoyne, a London estate agent, who bought The Firs, Southside, from Harris in 1907 for £420. J.B. Harris also built the Market Place, Chalfont St Peter, in 1923. George Burgoyne died in 1935, but his interest in the Firs estate, including many rented properties, was retained by his trustees until 1945, when it was purchased by the Pearl Assurance Company. John Bullard

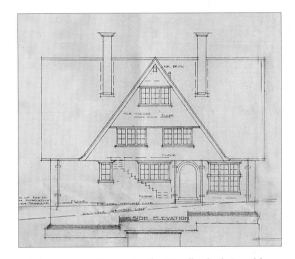

75 Chiltern House, 21 The Woodlands, designed by Arnold Mitchell for E.G. Eardley-Wilmot, 1907.

Harris moved to the Turret House, Packhorse Road, and died in 1956, leaving £80,000. The architect of most of the houses on The Firs estate was Leonard P. Kerkham, of Horning, Austenwood Common, formerly a partner in Kerkham, Burgess & Myers. His style did not change over the 30 years during which the estate was built, so some of his houses built in the late 1920s look remarkably similar to the early houses.

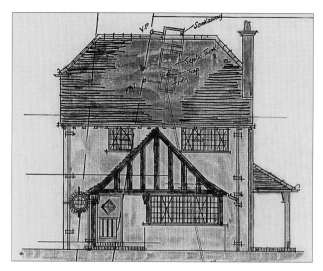

76 Sarum, 17 The Queensway, designed by Leonard P. Kerkham for George Burgoyne, 1928.

Latchmoor Estate

The Latchmoor estate was developed by the London & Country Investment & Property Company, of 11 Queen Victoria Street, London EC. In 1907, their surveyor at Gerrards Cross, Sydney Prevost, published a brochure called *Live in the Country*, in which he offered detached houses with large gardens from £950, or houses built to order to customer's own choice of design and plan. He went on to make some remarkably bold predictions about the growth of Gerrards Cross.

> The rate at which Gerrards Cross is being developed for residential purposes indicates that its health-giving and other advantages are being fully realised, and there is every reason to believe that the district will, in the course of a very few years, become the most important and popular high-class residential area on this side of the metropolis. One competent authority states that there will be a population of five thousand within two or three years, and, having in mind all the potentialities of the district, this does not seem to be in any way an exaggeration. And the mention of that large number need not be taken as evidence that the district will become congested, or its rural delights spoiled, for the class of residences that are being erected, and the way in which the estates are being laid out, precludes that possibility. In fact, the general outcome of the development will be a Rural Suburb.[11]

The London & Country Investment & Property Company purchased their land from James and William Gurney in 1906. It comprised both sides of Latchmoor Avenue, Latchmoor Grove, and the section of Orchehill Avenue between Oval Way and Latchmoor Avenue. The property portfolio seems to have been transferred to the New London & County Building & Estates Company about 1910. Both these property companies were closely connected with J.C. Richards & Co., builders, of Croxley Road, Paddington, who laid out the roads and sewers for the Latchmoor estate and built many of the houses there. The firm established a branch builder's yard in Station Road. Many of the houses built on the Latchmoor estate were designed by Sidney Prevost himself. One of his houses, Briarhedge, 33 Orchehill Avenue, features in a later edition of *Live in the Country*, published in 1910. Wisteria Cottage, 53 Orchehill Avenue, is a very similar design.

In 1918, the property developer, George Burgoyne, bought a plot of land to the west of The Firs estate from the lord of the manor, the Rev. Cyril Ashton Glover Moore. In 1924, Burgoyne also purchased the remaining landholdings of the New London & County Building and Estates Company, which was then in receivership. Although the building plots were not developed in his lifetime, Burgoyne's successors were able to lay out Latchmoor Way on this land. The first houses, such as The White Gate, 30 Latchmoor Way, were built in the late 1930s, but the bulk of the houses were built in the 1950s and 1960s.

Milton Park

In July 1891, the executors of Hugh Budgen Peake, the former owner of Maltman's Green Farm, auctioned 27 acres of land on the east side of Bull Lane. There were seven lots, each 'suitable for the erection of a gentleman's country residence'.[12] These were never built

77 The Latchmoor estate viewed from the other side of the railway cutting, about 1908.

78 The Square House, 5 Latchmoor Grove, built by the London & Country Investment & Property Company, 1908.

79 Sidney Prevost designed this house on the Latchmoor estate in 1909. It is now called Briarhedge, 33 Orchehill Avenue.

but, after the opening of the railway in 1906, some of this land was developed as the Milton Park estate. The developers were Archibald James Trace and Percy Wishart, who were 'turf commission agents' in Jermyn Street, London. Archibald Trace may have been advised to invest in Gerrards Cross by the estate agent, Herbert George Trace, of The Hawthorns, Austenway, who was probably a relative. The development was promoted by George Herbert, estate agent, from his office on Station Approach, Gerrards Cross. The Milton Park estate was advertised in the publication *Where to Live Round London*, in 1908.

> Excellent freehold building sites are offered on the Milton Park Estate, which occupies the choicest position on the outskirts of the district, yet being well within 10 minutes' easy walking-distance of the station. The estate stands upon high ground, is well away from the main and much-frequented roads, and is bounded by a picturesque old parish road. It overlooks two fine old parks, and is midway between Gerrard's Cross and Austenwood Commons, the latter of which it adjoins. Gas, water, and electric light are laid on. Gravel soil. Freehold or leasehold houses specially designed to suit purchasers' or tenants' requirements.
>
> For full particulars apply Percy A. Hopkins, architect, Milton Park Estate Office, Station Approach, Gerrards Cross.

Early development of the Milton Park estate centred on the west part of Orchehill Avenue and the north part of Milton Avenue at its junction with Bull Lane. It was not until the 1920s that Milton Avenue was joined to Orchehill Avenue and the development completed. Archibald James Trace lived at Milton Lodge, Milton Avenue, and later at Hayden, Orchehill Avenue. He died at Canford Cliffs, near Bournemouth, in 1946.

Austenwood Common

Austenwood Common is wholly within the parish of Chalfont St Peter, but the large country houses built around the Common in the period 1906 to 1914 form a more natural boundary to Gerrards Cross than the official boundary halfway down Oval Way. A major development next to the Common was controlled by the architect Edgar Ranger, who purchased a large

81   Churston, Bull Lane, designed by Percy Hopkins, was one of the first houses to be built on the Milton Park estate in 1907.

80 The White Gate, 30 Latchmoor Way, *c*.1939.

82   Brackenhurst, 91 Orchehill Avenue, designed by Paul Badcock, ARIBA, 1922.

EAST   ELEVATION TO ROAD

83 The Downs, Austenwood Lane, designed by Edgar Ranger, appeared in the *Studio Yearbook of Decorative Art*, 1912.

84 Old Basing, Austenwood Lane, designed by Edgar Ranger, 1912, and appearing in the *Studio Yearbook of Decorative Art*, 1913.

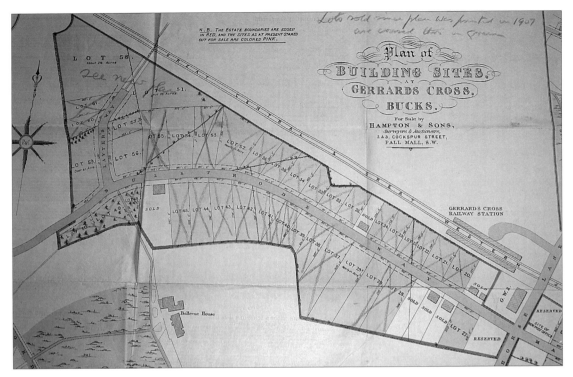

85 Plan of the building plots on Bulstrode Way marketed by Hampton & Sons, 1907.

plot of land near School Lane. He built The Downs and Kinnerton (now Craiglea House) in 1911, Old Basing, 1912, Kaduna, 1915, and Cottered, 1919. The *Three Pidgeons* was also rebuilt in the prevailing Arts and Crafts style in the 1930s. Another significant landmark is St Joseph's Roman Catholic Church, Austenwood Lane, begun in 1913 to the designs of Percy Lamb. In common with All Saints Church, Oval Way, the original building was conceived as only part of a larger project which was not completed until the 1960s.

South of the Railway

The area immediately south of the railway was developed by the estate agent George Hampton with his partners in Hampton, Gilks and Moon. They applied to Eton RDC for approval of new roads on 9 January 1906. This was a week before the land south of the new railway cutting was conveyed to them by

James and William Gurney, and nearly a month before the Gurneys held the first auction of their own building plots. Hampton, Gilks and Moon also purchased Marsham Farm from the successors of Henry Dolan, and land near Latchmoor Pond from trustees of Thomas Samworth. They immediately laid out building plots on Bulstrode Way and Marsham Way and made their first application for building regulations approval for two semi-detached houses on Marsham Way on 27 January. These two houses, Charnwood and Eastgrove, 33-35 Marsham Way, were therefore the first to be built in Gerrards Cross following the opening of the railway.

Bulstrode Way

Bulstrode Way was laid out in January 1906 by Messrs Hampton, Gilks and Moon. They bought the land in three parcels. The section nearest to Latchmoor Pond was acquired from

86   New houses on Bulstrode Way, 1910.

the successors of Thomas Samworth, one-time owner of Latchmoor Villa, later known as Waterside. The title to the second plot was traced back to George Spencer Smith, a former owner of Marsham Lodge. The remainder was bought from James and William Gurney, developers of the Orchehill estate, 17 January 1906. They laid out about 35 building plots along the new road, the largest of which extended to nearly one acre.

Hampton, Gilks and Moon had already made an application to Eton RDC for approval of new roads on 9 January 1906. They sold most of their building plots to well-to-do clients who employed their own architects and builders. Several houses were, however, built by speculative builders, notably by Henry Geeves and Albert H. James, both of Uxbridge, and the London & Country Investment & Property Co. The first building regulations application for houses in Bulstrode Way was made in April 1906, for three small but elegant detached

houses on the south side of the road, near to its junction with Packhorse Road. The applicant was a Londoner, John Stewart Young, who was probably building them to rent. In the event, only two were built, now numbered 17-19 Bulstrode Way, the third plot remaining vacant until 1908. In June 1906, the architects Hooper & Nash, of High Wycombe, applied to erect a small house and office (now demolished) opposite Mr Young's houses. In December 1906, an application was made by William George Blackmore to build a large house with stables on a one-acre plot next to Latchmoor Pond. Blackmore had a London address, but his family already rented Corheen, a genteel house on the Oxford Road, near to the *French Horn*. He was probably the first owner-occupier in Bulstrode Way. He called his new house Garston Lodge, but it is now known as Harewood, 55 Bulstrode Way.

George Hampton was slow to sell his building plots in Bulstrode Way for there were only five further applications to build houses in the road in 1907. These included a rather old-fashioned detached house built by Hooper & Nash next to their office. This house became known as Ingleside, 2 Bulstrode Way. Another early house, which looks old-fashioned compared with later development, is Rivendale, 20 Bulstrode Way, which was built to let in 1907 for Thomas N. Browne. These two houses, along with the three houses built in 1906, are marked as 'sold' on an undated plan of property for sale by Hampton & Sons.[13] The only notable house built in Bulstrode Way in 1907 was designed by the London architects, Fair & Myer, for Vice-Admiral Martin Julius Dunlop. The admiral named his house The Cottage, but it is now known as The Haven.

Development of Bulstrode Way really got under way in 1908 when 22 applications for building regulations approval were submitted. Amongst these were four unusual houses, designed by Fair & Myer, who were probably recommended by George Hampton when he sold the building plots. These were Roseleigh, 24 Bulstrode Way, built for Miss Shannon; Rondebosche (now Holmbury), 28 Bulstrode Way, for Alfred Robinson; Feltrim Lodge (now Blewbury House), 51 Bulstrode Way, for Col Fagan; and Wiltshire House (later Levelis and now Allendale), 53 Bulstrode Way, for Major Amesbury.

Three plots on Bulstrode Way were purchased from Hamptons by the London & Country Investment & Property Company. Sydney Prevost designed their houses, one of which, West Lodge, 48 Bulstrode Way, appeared in the 1908 advertising brochure entitled *Live in the Country*. This house is unremarkable, but Wyke House and Bulstrode House, 50 and 52 Bulstrode Way, are better examples of Prevost's work, featuring his signature double bay windows beneath partially hipped gables.

87 Fremar (now Rosemullion), 42 Bulstrode Way, built *c*.1908 for Col Frederick Walter Danter.

88   Orchard Leigh, now Little Orchards, Layters Way, designed by Johnson & Boddy.

The remaining plots in Bulstrode Way were gradually built on, with five new houses in 1909. The best of these, and probably the finest piece of architecture in the road, was Oldhurst, designed by the distinguished architect, P. Morley Horder, for Edward Rouse.[14] Three further houses followed in 1910, one in 1911, two in 1912, one in 1913 and two in 1915. Two late additions were The Hollies, 15 Bulstrode Way, designed by Edgar Ranger for W. Payne in 1920, and Stapleton, 31 Bulstrode Way, built to the plans of C. W. Clark for Percy Clayton in 1923.

Layters Way

The first section of Layters Way, from Bulstrode Way to the footbridge over the railway, was developed by Hampton, Gilks and Moon on land purchased from Mrs Samworth of Latchmoor Villa, later Waterside. It contains several notable houses, including Layters Cottage and Cranford, designed by Fair & Myer in 1908 and 1909 respectively, and Orchard Leigh, by Johnson & Boddy, built in 1909. The best is undoubtedly Old Tile House, designed by Kemp & How for Robert Lawton Tate, an insurance underwriter, in 1910.[15]

The extension of Layters Way to Bull Lane was laid out by the surveyor, George F. Duck, for the builder, Claude Baldwin.[16] The land was purchased in 1914 from Mrs Edith Laura Wordley, wife of Thomas Wordley, of Bull Mead, Bull Lane. Baldwin & Duck built seven houses in Layters Way between 1914 and 1920.

Marsham Way

Marsham Way was laid out by Hampton, Gilks & Moon on land formerly belonging to Marsham Farm. The first building regulations applications relating to Marsham Way were for semi-detached houses, suggesting that the developers were not sure of their market. The earliest was in January 1906, when plans were submitted by George Hampton himself, for two houses now known as Charnwood and Eastgrove, 33-35 Marsham Way. The architect was Ernest W. Banfield. Hampton & Son submitted plans for another pair of semi-detached houses, again by Banfield, in April 1906. These are now Quendon Cottage and Hestia, 43-45 Marsham Way. A plot for two more semi-detached houses was bought by

Albert H. James of Uxbridge, builder. His plans were prepared by the architect, William L. Eves, also of Uxbridge, and submitted in August 1906. These houses are now Southcote and Little Silver, 37-41 Marsham Way.

There was only one house built in Marsham Way in 1907. This was a superior house called The Rowans, now 22 Marsham Way, designed for the builder, John Bailey, by Kirkham, Burgess & Myers.[17] There were no applications relating to Marsham Way in 1908, but there were eight in 1909. Three of these were built by Henry Geeves of Uxbridge and designed by Johnson &

89 Marsham Way, *c.*1950.

90 The Wyke, 16 Marsham Way, extended for Catherine Porter, 1920.

91 Marsham Farm, now known as Marsham Manor, rebuilt to the designs of Stanley Hamp, 1907.

Boddy, who had also designed some of Geeves's houses in Bulstrode Way. These were Pinecote, 6-8 Marsham Way, The Wyke, 16 Marsham Way, and Marsham Cottage, 20 Marsham Way.

There were four houses built in Marsham Way in 1910, two of which were owned and built by Y.J. Lovell & Son and designed by Johnson & Boddy. These were Lynton, 27 Marsham Way, and Merton, 29 Marsham Way. Of the seven houses built in Marsham Way in 1911 five of them were by Y.J. Lovell & Son, with Johnson & Boddy as the architects. These included Burghley Place, 19 Marsham Way, Studley Lodge, 25 Marsham Way, Culverkeys, 2-4 Marsham Way and Blandings, on the corner of Fulmer Way.

The 1907 Hampton estate map shows Marsham Farm, on the corner of Marsham Way and Marsham Lane, as already sold. It had been bought by Tibbs & Co., builders, of Wembley, and rebuilt to the design of Stanley Hamp. The design featured a new corridor across the front of the house, linking an old wing on the north-west to a new Arts and Crafts-inspired wing on the south-west. In 1907, the same architect designed a house called Abbotsmead, on the other side of Marsham Way, with similarly generous timbered gables and tall chimneys.[18]

Some larger houses were built on the extension to Marsham Way, between Marsham Lane and Mill Lane. Badminton House, 38 Marsham Way, was built in 1913 for William E. Preston, a leading bank manager, to the designs of Messrs Wood, Sarvis & Muir. Montrose, 43 Marsham Way, was designed by Sydney Prevost, also in 1913. The Holt, 75 Marsham Way, was built in 1920 for Mrs Hornibrook, to the design of A. Hannaford, architect, Gerrards Cross. Perhaps the most elegant house in the road is Arkley, 69 Marsham Way, designed in 1922 by Robert Muir for Robert Snare, a London milliner.[19]

Fulmer Way

Quakers Way, or Fulmer Way as it was later called, was built on land purchased from the owners of Marsham Farm by Hampton, Gilks & Moon. This was a popular road as some of the gardens were large and backed on to Gerrards Cross Common. Of the 13 houses built in the period 1909-14, 11 were designed by Johnson & Boddy, and eight were built by Y.J. Lovell & Son. The first house to be built was L'Abri, now known as Doulma, 11 Fulmer Way, in 1909. It was designed by Johnson & Boddy for A.C. Frost and built by Claude Baldwin, of Gerrards

Cross. It featured in the architectural press at the time.[20] The most elegant of the houses is perhaps Heathside, 12 Fulmer Way, which was designed by Davis & Boddy in 1914. It is best viewed from the rear, where two handsome gables overlook Gerrards Cross Common.

Vicarage Way

Vicarage Way was laid out by Hampton, Gilks & Moon on land formerly part of Marsham Farm. The building plots were as generous as in the neighbouring extension to Marsham Way. The first plot to be taken was for Dinthill, a large detached house designed by R.H. Ernest Hill ARIBA, in 1909 for John William Western.[21] It is now a nursing home called Howard House. The architect Sidney Prevost developed four of the plots in Vicarage Way, probably for the London & Country Investment & Property Co. The Barton, 18

Vicarage Way, built in 1912, is a larger version of Prevost's houses at 33 and 53 Orchehill Avenue. Kingston House, 20 Vicarage Way, built in 1912, is similar to his double bow-windowed houses at 50 and 52 Bulstrode Way. Wychwood, 15 Vicarage Way, built in 1913, is a superior version of West Lodge, 48 Bulstrode Way. The largest and most elegant of Prevost's houses in Gerrards Cross is Oaklands, 7 Vicarage Way, dating from 1913.

The Common

Whilst the surveyors and builders were laying out new roads with building plots for large houses, more modest development was taking place around Gerrards Cross Common. In 1907, Thomas Westacott of The Greenway, Uxbridge, builder, who was born in Devon, built a terrace of four houses called Devon Villas near Latchmoor Pond, and renamed two existing cottages there

92 Somersby, 22 Fulmer Way, designed by Johnson & Boddy, 1911.

93   Howard House, Vicarage Way designed by R.H. Ernest Hill for John W. Western, 1909.

as Devon Cottages. In 1908, James Langstone built four cottages called Langstone Villas, near the *Packhorse Inn*, to the design of William Eves of Uxbridge. These were more substantial than the earlier cottages on the Common, being valued in 1912 at £320 each, including land. F.H. Bonsey built the house next to his butcher's shop on East Common, calling it Brindgwood House. In 1912, the local builder, John Bailey, put up 18 cottages near the *French Horn*, calling his new street Pinewood Close.[22] In the same year he built two semi-detached houses on Oxford Road, called Boscombe and Woodside.

The Paddock House, designed by the leading London architects Forbes & Tate for the solicitor, J. Stewart-Wallace, set a much higher tone. It was followed by the neighbouring Widenham House, also designed by Forbes & Tate, in 1911. The building of large houses on the south side of Oxford Road got under way with the release of land from the Bulstrode estate in the mid-1920s. Henry Brown & Co., now of 1 Westbury Road, London W2, built several houses here between 1925 and 1930.

This ribbon development along the Oxford Road continued throughout the 1930s.

Houses on the Common had become particularly desirable. William Phillimore even went as far as giving the Common as his address, even though he actually lived at Moranside, Bulstrode Way. For others, renting on the Common was a first step into the area. For example, J.E. Thomas was listed in 1917 in the Old Post Office, but by 1924 was living in Lavenders, Bull Lane. In the 1907 *Kelly's Directory*, there were 16 private residents living around the Common, in houses built well before 1906. By 1924 there were 17 private residents listed for the Common. Despite the construction of a number of major houses between then and 1924, the number of private residents listed in the 1924 directory was approximately the same. This may reflect the fact that some houses were aging. The largest change in the appearance of housing round the Common was, however, not the infilling that had occurred between 1876 and 1938, but the demolition of the group of four major Victorian houses, including Heathfield, in the early 1960s, and the construction instead of the Bulstrode Court flats.

Woodhill Estate

At the sale of the Woodhill estate in 1923, Lot 6, 50 acres of building land, was purchased in 1923 by Clifford Percy Lovell for £12,905. The roads were laid out in 1923 by Kennard and Kennard, architects and surveyors, of 12 Grays Inn Square, London WC1.[23] Y.J. Lovell & Son gradually developed the plots, sometimes using their own drawing office to produce the plans, but in many cases employing Douglas Tanner, the architect who designed many of the firm's houses for the Ideal Home Exhibitions. The Glen House, 37 Woodhill Avenue, featured in the Ideal Home Exhibition in 1926. The best houses on the Woodhill estate are designed by another architect favoured by Y.J. Lovell & Son, A.L. Abbott. He designed the three houses on Woodhill Avenue now called Winridge, Sandene and The Bumbles, built by Y.J. Lovell & Son in 1935.

Dukes Wood Estate

Sir John Ramsden began to develop the Dukes Wood estate in the late 1920s. A booklet was

94 The Paddock House, West Common, designed by Forbes & Tate, 1914.

95   The Glen House, 37 Woodhill Avenue, designed by Douglas G. Tanner & Arthur L. Horsburgh, 1926.

issued describing the 364 acres for sale, with frontages of about 1,000ft to Oxford Road, 4,400 ft to Windsor Road, and 3,290ft to Fulmer Road.[24] The land afforded 'magnificent sites for the erection of mansions, or for sub-division into lots to suit intending purchasers whose requirements are less ambitious, where moderate sized residences could be erected'. Hetherington & Secret, of Ealing, were the sole agents, but further particulars could be obtained from R.G. Baty, Bulstrode Estate Office, Gerrards Cross, or from W.J. Hetherington, Goodrest, Fulmer Way, Gerrards Cross. Robinson & Roods, surveyors, 37 Bedford Row, London WC2, drew up plans for Dukes Wood Avenue in 1926. The same firm developed many of the building plots,

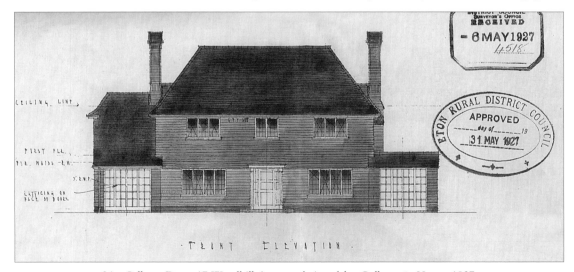

96   Callcott Dene, 17 Woodhill Avenue, designed by Collcutt & Hamp, 1927.

sometimes under their own name, and at other times as the Circle Land Company, or Ideal Homes Ltd. Over thirty houses had been built on Dukes Wood Avenue by 1932.

In 1932, Sir John Ramsden was forced to put the whole of the Bulstrode estate, extending to 815 acres, on the market. The sale was only a partial success, with 607 acres sold at £38,565 (i.e. £64 per acre). A number of the plots were withdrawn prior to the sale and many were not sold, including the house and park. On a surviving copy of the sale particulars, annotated in hand by the agent, prices of individual development plots are marked, ranging from £151 to £715 per acre, with an average of £350.

Lot 40, the remainder of Dukes Wood, was described as 200 acres of woodland bounded by the Windsor and Fulmer Roads. It was purchased by the Watson Investment Company, of Great Pednor Manor, Chesham. This firm laid out Dukes Wood Drive in 1936. Ten houses were built in 1937, two by Richmond Watson's Bulstrode Development Company, and

97 Cornerways, 38 Mill Lane, designed by F.C. Moscrop-Young FRIBA, 1928.

four by W.H. Price, builder, Station Approach, Gerrards Cross. The development of Dukes Wood Drive continued after the Second World War with William Old Ltd, builders of Watford, developing many of the plots.

Windsor Road

Windsor Road was largely developed after 1932 as part of the Dukes Wood estate. One of the best houses in this ribbon development

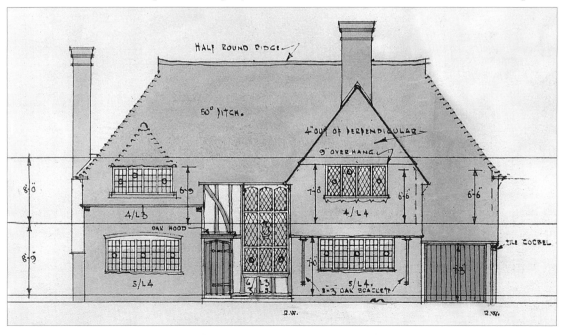

98 The Bumbles, 8 Woodhill Avenue, designed by A.L. Abbott for Y.J. Lovell & Son, 1935.

99   Dukes Wood Avenue, *c.*1935.

is Winnards Perch, 47 Windsor Road, designed by J. Stanley Beard in 1934. Before the sale of the Bulstrode estate in 1932, however, Sir John Ramsden's agents had laid out several building plots along Windsor Road. Lots 41-3 in the sale comprised nine building plots, each with a frontage of over 100ft to Windsor Road, near its junction with Hedgerley Lane. One of these plots was acquired by Cyril Mervyn White, who employed Prentice & Partners to design Timbercombe, an ultra-modern house with plain white walls, flat roof, and a dramatic curved staircase window. The house was built by Y.J. Lovell & Son in 1936. Cyril Mervyn White was a racing driver who died following a crash in his Bugatti in practice for the international car race at Cork in May 1937.

Several of the building plots on Windsor Road were purchased by Stanley Hamp, of architects Collcutt & Hamp. Here he built several houses in the modern style, although they are brick-built and rendered rather than

100   Dukes Mead, Manor Lane, designed by J. Stanley Beard, 1928

101 Felbrigg, Fulmer Road, built in 1931 for G.N. Rouse from the designs of W.S. Grice & Dennis Poulton. Felbrigg has now been demolished and replaced by a cul-de-sac of houses called Elmwood Park.

102 One of the house designs used by William Old Ltd, builders of Watford, in Dukes Wood Drive, 1957.

constructed in concrete. Some of these houses have now been demolished, but most have had their flat roofs changed to pitched roofs, detracting from their architectural impact. Casa Blanca, 105 Windsor Road, built in 1934, does, however, still have its flat roof.

Camp Road

Before the sale of the Bulstrode estate in 1932, the land around Bulstrode Camp had been earmarked for a golf course. In 1934, Sir John Ramsden sold 263 acres north-west of the camp for £19,989 to the Watson Investment Company.[26] This firm was based at Great Pednor Manor, Chesham, and run by Richmond Watson. His company submitted

plans of Valley Way and Top Park in 1936, and Main Drive in 1937.[27] Several of the houses built on these roads were built for the Bulstrode Development Company, also of Great Pednor Manor, but later operating from site offices at the Bull Lodge. The old established firm of architects, Burgess, Holden & Watson, of Beaconsfield, were closely linked to these companies.

Council Housing

Eton Rural District Council began building council houses after the First World War, employing Julian Burgess of Burgess, Holden & Watson, Beaconsfield, as their architect. A plot of land south-west of Fulmer Road, formerly

103 Winnards Perch, 47 Windsor Road, designed by J. Stanley Beard, 1934.

104 Timbercombe, now called White Gables, 77 Windsor Road, designed for Cyril Mervyn White, by Prentice & Partners, 1936.

LOVELL BUILT   GERRARDS CROSS
Messrs. COLLCUTT & HAMP, F/F.R.I.B.A., *Architects.*

105   Gosmore, 111 Windsor Road, designed by Stanley Hamp, 1934.

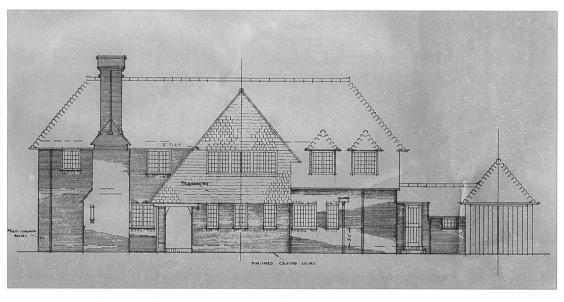

106   Garden Reach, Camp Road, designed for Mrs Hutchison by Robert G. Muir, 1935.

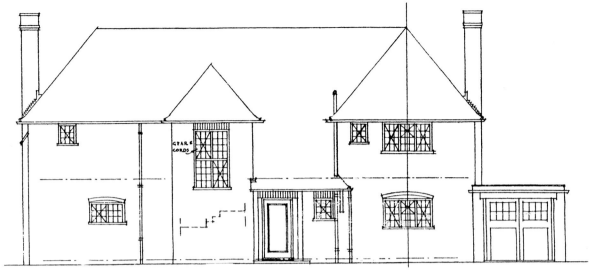

107 Stoneygate, Top Park, designed by Burgess, Holden & Watson, for the Bulstrode Development Co., 1936.

108 Old Tyles, Camp Road, designed by A.L. Abbott, 1936.

109   Council houses at Gaviots Green, Fulmer Road, *c.*1955.

belonging to Col William Le Poer Trench, was secured, with space for 50 houses. Gerrards Cross Parish Council formed a Housing Committee to review applications, with instructions to favour ex-servicemen. In the event, only 16 houses were built, these being completed in 1922. The new road was named Gaviots Way.

The remainder of the road was later developed for private housing. Further council houses were built after the Second World War. These were on the north-east side of Fulmer Road, with 36 houses at Gaviots Green and 44 at Gaviots Close.

Seven

The Newcomers

When the new houses and shops which had sprung up beside Gerrards Cross Station were barely ten years old, a directory was published, listing the names of the new residents, and the tradesmen who served them. The directory must have been successful, for in 1921 a much fuller version was published. The editor explained that during the intervening three years, although hardly any new houses had been built, nearly 250 new residents had replaced others, and the names of 50 houses had been changed. The new edition included a street-by-street list of all the houses in the order in which they appeared along each street. So that the newcomers could locate their friends, and tradesmen could locate their customers, the directory even provided an alphabetical index of the house names, giving the street in which each house could be found. House names like Bella Vista and Sunnyside reflected the optimism of the new residents; Clovelly and Tresco suggested that the situation was every bit as attractive as a favoured holiday resort; and Kenilworth and Runnymede showed a pride in English history somewhat at odds with life in a new town. Even more pretentious were those who included their own surname in the name of their house, such as Arthur Hope Smith, of Hopetown House, North Park, and Frederick Noble Jones of Jonesboro, Packhorse Road.

What motivated so many upper-middle-class London families to start a new life in Gerrards Cross? The lure of the Chiltern landscape was strong. An estate agent enthused that:

Gerrards Cross stands 300 feet above sea level, on the edge of the Chiltern Hills, amidst beautifully beech-wooded scenery and on gravel soil. In the neighbourhood are beautiful heather and furze clad commons and lovely park lands and woods, and within a short distance are many places abounding in historical and literary interest. There is an excellent service of trains to both Marylebone and Paddington, some of which perform the journey in 25 minutes. The business man is well catered for and there is also a theatre train provided every night. First class golf, hunting, fishing and boating are also obtainable within a few miles.[1]

Another estate agent claimed that:

Gerrards Cross is reputed to be one of the choicest residential localities within an 18 mile radius of the north west of town. The neighbourhood is unknown to the motor omnibus and the tripper element and is in simple language a high class residential neighbourhood. The climate is superlatively healthy, the soil being gravel, the air is bracing and the district is known as the Brighton of Bucks. All residences of a first-class nature. Good society. Hunting: His Majesty's Stag Hounds and also the Old Berkeley hunt the district with the former meeting in Gerrards Cross.[2]

The romance of commons was certainly one of the attractions. This was reflected in land values, with sites facing either Gerrards Cross or Austenwood Common commanding a premium in 1912. Constance Maynard, former Mistress of Westfield College and a resident of Marsham Way from 1924 to 1935, gave her recreation as short bicycling tours. William Phillimore was also a keen cyclist.

The major reason for moving to Gerrards Cross was probably the combination of country

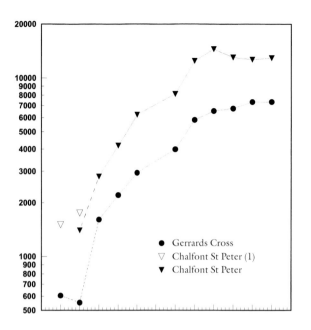

Gerrards Cross Population 1901-2001

The growth of the population of Gerrards Cross as defined in this book cannot be readily taken from the census reports, as so much of the area lay in Chalfont St Peter. Figures for the two parishes between 1901 and 2001 show much the same growth pattern. The percentage growth rate was higher in Gerrards Cross from 1901-11, but thereafter Gerrards Cross only outgrew Chalfont St Peter in the 1931-51 period, with its expansion south of Gerrards Cross Common on the Dukes Wood and Camp Road estates.

Gerrards Cross Population 1891-2001				
			% Change	
	GX	CSP	GX	CSP
1891	605	1509		
1901	552	1753 (1402)*		
1911	1612	2802	192	100
1921	2208	4183	37	49
1931	2942	6217	33	49
1951	3988	8,114	36	31
1961	5821	12460	46	54
1971	6524	14498	12	16
1981	6739	13027	3	-10
1991	7337	12669	9	-3
2001	7342	12937	0	2

* boundary change; 1402 relates to the extent of the parish in 1911

air and suburban facilities. The reliable train service, the new sewage system, and the availability of mains water, gas and electricity, made Gerrards Cross particularly suitable to families. This was reflected in the number of private schools which were established in Gerrards Cross. In view of the covenants in the deeds to most residential properties, it is surprising that most of the schools operated, at least at first, from ordinary houses. In 1914, Cranley Court School, in North Park, was advertising in *The Times*. It seems that the school did not survive long after 1921. Even shorter-lived was a High School for girls at North Park in 1917, but it may have moved to Maltmans Green shortly afterwards. By 1929 Innisfree School was operating from another house in North Park. The demand for school spaces can be seen in the history of Gayhurst School, which started in Milton Avenue, and then moved to its new premises by 1924. Thorpe House School was purpose-built in 1925. Chalfont Lodge was a school from 1931. St Mary's School appears in 1938.

The census figures for the number of households in Gerrards Cross parish show this growth even more dramatically: 218 households were added in the period 1901-11, 144 from 1911-21, 234 from 1921-31, 383 from 1931-51, and 643 from 1951-61.

In the period 1906 to 1940, the London upper middle class was dominated by the higher professions, particularly law, medicine, the Army and the upper echelons of the Civil Service. Gerrards Cross was to gain many residents from these groups. Businessmen like Harold Sanderson of The Tudors, South Park Crescent, were less common, and were less likely to appear in *The Times*.[3] As men established in their professions, many arrived in Gerrards Cross in their 40s or 50s. Some were older and seem to have come to Gerrards Cross to retire.

The quality of the residents can be seen during emergencies. In the First World War there was a War Hospital Supply Depot in Gerrards Cross, manned by volunteers. During the General Strike, in 1926, 60 men came forward as special constables, and 200 as general volunteers. An upper-middle-class area was not immune to problems that faced all classes in the period, however. In 1938 J. Moore, aged 82, and his wife, aged 49, of The Gables, Fulmer Way, died of flu in the same week.

Law

The upper echelons of the law were not as well represented in Gerrards Cross as might have been expected, perhaps because the journey from Paddington to the Inns of Court was not as easy as that from Charing Cross. In 1911, however, W.M. Leycester, a metropolitan magistrate, lived at Masson End, The Woodlands, and in the same road was Edward Eardley-Wilmot, later to be a Bencher of Lincoln's Inn. By 1915, they had been joined by John Stewart-Wallace, who was to be Lord Justice of Appeal, 1929-40. Others arrived between 1920 and 1940, including Dr D. Cotes-Preedy, who was qualified both medically and as a barrister, and was vice president of the Legal Medical Society. Some came to Gerrards Cross to retire. They included, in 1938, Sir Archibald McDonald Gordon, who as a barrister had been formerly Counsellor and Labour Attaché at the British Embassy, Washington. Another was His Honour Frank Sewell Cooper, Judge of the Mayor's and City of London Court.

Medicine

There was a greater representation of leaders in the medical profession, probably reflecting the ease of access to Harley Street and major hospitals in the West End. In general there were a substantial number of residents with medical qualifications, with the more junior having been attracted to an area with affluent patients. At the head of the medical group of residents was Maj. Gen. T.W. Gibbard, who was Hon. Surgeon to the King. Sir William Kershaw, the King's Coroner, was resident from 1921 to 1940, and was himself operated on for appendicitis at his home at Walton Cottage, Oval Way. Another doctor who lived in Oval Way was D. Moir-Byres, a Harley Street consultant with a post at the London Homeopathic Hospital. Dr Cotes-Preedy was a neighbour of both. Dame Louise McIlroy was Professor of Obstetrics and Gynaecology at the University of London and the Royal Free Hospital, London. Others included Gilbert Haywood Howells, Consulting Surgeon at the Royal National Ear, Nose and Throat Hospital; Edward Philip Stibbe, Professor of Anatomy, University of London, King's College; William Wright, Dean and Professor of Anatomy in the Medical College, London Hospital; and Percival Macleod Yearsley, Senior Surgeon to the Royal Ear Hospital.

Academic

Gerrards Cross also attracted its share of university professors. The railway to Paddington was apparently an attractive route for those working at Imperial College, as there was only a mile's walk across Kensington Gardens to the College. As a result of this Gerrards Cross may have housed more Fellows of the Royal Society than any small settlement in the country. In the period 1928-31 there were three in residence at the same time, Professor Baker, resident at Latchmoor House from 1911 to 1935, Professor Percy Groom at Pinehurst, North Park from 1911 to 1931, and Professor Patrick Buxton, at Grit Howe, South Park Crescent from 1928. Other academics attracted to the area included C.C. Fortescue, Professor of Electrical Engineering at Imperial College, resident at Uplands, Marsham Way 1928-33.

Such intellectual accomplishment was not limited to men. Constance Maynard, former Mistress of Westfield College, was probably only the peak of the female brain power. Professor Baker's wife was a chemist in her own right and shared a laboratory with her husband at Latchmoor House. She devised an improved chemical agent used in respirators supplied to Allied troops to protect them from poisoned gas during the First World War. In July 1915 she worked on an antiseptic khaki dye used for army field dressings. She was one of the few women from Gerrards Cross appearing in the *Ladies' Who's Who* in 1924.[4]

Military

The expansion of the Army prior to and during the First World War led to an increase in the establishment of the War Office. Gerrards Cross was well placed to house senior officers, but many of those who came did so for only a short time, given the mobility required of officers. In 1911, 1915 and 1917, the directories listed 36 officers, although some of them would have been retired. Nevertheless, only four were recorded in more than one of these directories. Some houses had successive military residents. Thus at Danecourt, North Park, in 1911, there was a Lt J.H.F. Cole and in 1915 a Maj. Gen. Shakespear. Other than the retired Maj. Gen. Prior, at Ethorpe, there were three generals in Gerrards Cross: Gen. A.S. Collard, in School Lane; Lt Gen. Pearse at Fairoak, North Park; and Surgeon Gen. Barrington at Oakfield, North Park. Another medical officer was Surgeon Commander G. Dickenson, living at Bawdsley, Milton Avenue. Rear Admiral Boyle at Elmshurst, Bulstrode Way, was the senior naval officer. Other naval officers were Engineer Commander Croisdale at Maryland, Bulstrode Way and J.B. White, of Alderbourne Manor, who, as Assistant Director of Naval Recruiting during the First World War, took the rank of Captain. Additionally there were at least seven captains, six majors and 12 colonels. Amongst the retired army officers were some early arrivals: Colonel Fagan at Feltrim Lodge, and his neighbour Major Amesbury, at Wiltshire House, Bulstrode Way, who had both retired from the Indian Army.

The Civil Service

The upper levels of the Civil Service were well represented in Gerrards Cross. There were several civil servant knights. John Stewart-Wallace, Chief Land Registrar, moving to Milton Avenue, Gerrards Cross, in 1911, and then to The Paddock House, West Common, in 1914. W.B. Blatch, of North Park, was Solicitor to the Inland Revenue. H.W. Malkin, of The Barton, Vicarage Way, was Legal Adviser to the Foreign Office. Alfred Robinson was Deputy Secretary of the Ministry of Transport. Others included Thomas Deeves, Assistant Secretary at the Ministry of Food and the Foreign Office and Walter Henry Guillebaud, Deputy Director General of the Forestry Commission.

The Arts

The Arts were well represented in Gerrards Cross. Living on West Common was Frederick Cullen, a landscape artist. Another painter was Joseph Barnard Davis, resident in The Ridgway. As was the case with many newly arrived residents during the First World War, Bruce Frederick Cummings, resident of Kingsway, diarist and biologist, and perhaps a member of staff at the Natural History Museum, had expressed concerns that his writings might perish in a Zeppelin raid. Sir Granville Bantock was resident in The Ridgway from 1938. Miss Gertrude Gregory of Little Baddow, Orchehill Rise, was late Professor of Violin at the London Academy of Music and leader of Rene Ortmans' Wigmore Hall Orchestra, as well as a member of Henry Wood's Queen's Hall Orchestra. She accepted violin and piano pupils, as well as providing orchestral and ensemble classes and recitals 'at home'. It is probable that Ortmans lived at The Elms, The Woodlands, from where a Miss Marjorie Ortmans also gave piano tuition.

Colonial Civil Service

In the period 1906-1914, and after the First World War, retired senior colonial civil servants were another important component of the upper middle class. Gerrards Cross was very suitable for a full or semi retirement. David Keith Cunnison of Ravenscroft, Bulstrode Way, had been Secretary, Bengal Chamber of Commerce, Calcutta. Sir Meyrick Hewlett, of Two Gates, Orchehill Avenue, had been Consul-General in Hankow, 1931-35, and had served in the Consular Service from 1898 to 1937. Sir Henry Greene Kelly at The Gables, Marsham Lane, was a colonial judge who had retired in 1908. Sir John Kerr at Fairstead, Latchmoor Avenue, had been Governor of Assam. G.E. Soames of Bay House, North Park, had been Chief Secretary of Assam in 1925. Sir Herbert Pearson, at Levelis, Bulstrode Way, had been a High Court Judge at Calcutta, 1920-33, and then Legal Adviser to the Secretary of State, India Office, 1933-8, before coming to Gerrards Cross in 1938. Another who moved to Gerrards Cross by 1940 was E.J. Scott at Little Stover, Camp Road, who had been Chief Secretary, 1932-35, and then Acting Governor and Commander in Chief, Uganda. Some who had served abroad may have chosen Gerrards Cross because of a family connection. Claude Strickland was at Corner House, The Woodlands in 1924, and moved to Greenacre, Latchmoor Avenue. His father may have lived at Fairstead, Latchmoor Avenue, from 1915-24.

Businessmen

Sir Samuel Fay was the leading businessman to be associated with Gerrards Cross. Sam Fay's salary at this time was £3,000, placing him in the first rank of those who worked for a living.

Other senior businessmen are less easy to trace and tended to stay only a short time in Gerrards Cross. James Gomer Berry, later 1st Viscount Kemsley, lived at Granville, Vicarage Way, at the time when he was building his newspaper empire, acquiring the *Sunday Times* in 1915 and the *Financial Times* in 1919. William, 1st Baron Vestey, head of the meat empire, briefly lived at Cleeve Cottage, Bulstrode Way, before his death in 1940. Austin Reed was a longer-term resident, having moved to The Tudors, South Park Crescent, soon after it was built in 1921. His dressing room was fitted out with drawers fit for his Regent Street shop. He remained at The Tudors until moving to Garden Reach, Camp Road, where he died in 1954.

A number of residents held senior positions in banking and finance. They included Sir William Preston, of Badminton House, Marsham Way, Chief Manager Chartered Bank of India, Australia & China. M.A Jacques was a stockbroker and Member of Lloyds. Some were involved with the new industries which made West London so prosperous in the inter-war period. R.R. Rhodes was director, Blackburn Aircraft Co. A.A.D. Lang, of San Marco, held important air plane patents in the same industries. E.L Colston of St Bernard's, Oak End Way, was joint managing director of the Hoover Company. George Edward Howse, of Inveroaks, North Park, was a director of William Cooks. F.H.D. Button was chairman of Alfred Button & Co., of Uxbridge, a company with a variety of interests in the grocery trade, including Budgens and Holland & Barrett. G.N. Rouse of Felbrigg, Fulmer Road, was a Lloyds Underwriter and later a member of the Lloyds Council.

The Upper Classes

Before the opening of the railway, Gerrards Cross had been dominated by the main estates. After 1906 Bulstrode Park remained, but it is not clear how much it was used, as Sir John

Ramsden preferred Muncaster Castle near Ravenglass. However, there were still great occasions there. In 1925, Bulstrode Park was one of the few houses outside central London to hold a ball included in the Court Circular. Colonel Le Poer Trench's connections would have meant that he and his wife were in the same circle as Sir John. Another family who probably qualified were the Drummonds of Maltmans Green. They would have gained national and local fame when one of their seven children won a VC. The family were wealthy enough from their banking connections to have homes in St James's and Gerrards Cross.

There were a few new residents who had aristocratic backgrounds, but whether these were good enough for them to be invited to Bulstrode Park is again not known. It appears that even Professor Baker FRS, living in Latchmoor House, was not invited to the big house. Amongst local residents for whom an exception may have been made were the Eardley-Wilmots, who first took up residence at the Corner House, The Woodlands, and then succeeded Sir Sam Fay at Raylands Mead, Bull Lane, in 1924. Their daughter was presented at Court in 1924. Residents with a title included Major Lord Bury, later 9th Earl of Albemarle, at Camp House, Oxford Road in 1921; Lady Elphinstone Agnes Sugden, fifth daughter of the Earl of Montalt, at Mawd, Kingsway; Lady M.E. Clauson, who may have been in temporary residence at Gerrards Cross whilst Hawkshead House, North Mymms, was being renovated; and the Hon. Mrs Pelham, wife of the Hon. H.G.G. Pelham, second son of the 5th Earl Chichester, at Ivy Cottage, Lower Road. Among other residents who had attended or been presented at Court was Mrs Francis Goodbody, whose husband was at a King's Levee at St James's Palace in 1922. Lord Tredegar's daughter had lived in Gerrards Cross for nine or ten months but, for some reason, it did not suit her so she moved to Wimbledon. She later committed suicide and was found dead in the Thames.

The division between the upper class and the upper middle class so fully represented in Gerrards Cross can be seen from the entries in the *Ladies' Who's Who* of 1924. It contains only three entries for Gerrards Cross, whereas there were about 120 for Buckinghamshire as a whole, out of a national total of about 17,000. Thus, whilst Gerrards Cross had a slightly disproportionate number of such entries for the county, it was by no measure specially attractive to the upper classes at this date.

Geographical Origins

The newcomers seem predominantly to have come from London. Prior to the First World War, the owners' addresses given on the building regulations applications for new houses are often high status addresses in central or west London, mainly Ealing and Harrow, and some in Uxbridge. Between the wars the number from west London grew, with suburbs such as Pinner, Northwood, Ruislip and Hanwell being common. Some house names were brought with them by new residents. Sir William Preston's Badminton House was given the same name as his previous house in Finchley.

The movement from London to Gerrards Cross was not only one way. The Woodlands was developed mainly before 1914 and can be used as an example of the process. W. Haldane Porter, who built Quenby, The Woodlands, in 1906, gave his address as 54 Victoria Street, London. Porter was the Home Office Inspector of Aliens, a post which assumed great importance in 1914. After 1930 he left Gerrards Cross and moved to Dublin where he was a director of Arthur Guinness Son & Co. Anthony C. Meyjes, editor of the *Ironmonger*, was living in one of the first houses to be built in Austenway when his plan for Thornhyrst, The Woodlands, was submitted in 1908. He had moved to Ealing, however, before his death in 1925. Mrs Ada Kuhlenthal gave her address as Cann Road, Ealing, when applying to build Davan House, the Woodlands, in 1907. Her subsequent applications for further houses on the site are from Cambridge Terrace, Hyde Park, so she obviously spent only part of the year at Gerrards Cross.

Not all early residents were men of property. Both before and after the First World War the directories list many of the houses in the possession of spinsters and of married ladies, most of whom were probably widows. This may have had an influence on the sex ratio of the parish (see below). As early as 1912, an advert for superior apartments suitable for one or two ladies at Highfield, Milton Avenue, 23 miles from the West End, recommended them for health, and their moderate terms. In 1911 the Misses Cook were in residence, so perhaps they were seeking ladies to share their new house.

Local Businessmen

Many of the local retailers would have lived over their shops, others in Chalfont St Peter, which may in part have acted as a dormitory for Gerrards Cross. Robert Binder moved from Ealing to Station Parade and may have lived over his shop in 1921. He was at Breezemount, Austenway, from 1924-9, but then moved to a new house, Budarray, Dukes Wood Avenue. Another trader who had moved from Ealing in 1910, P.B. Spaull, prospered so that by 1920 he was investing in the construction of two houses in Orchehill Rise and was resident at Little Orme in 1929. Perhaps the biggest rise was that of the butcher, H.J. Bonsey, who was 41 in 1901. With the arrival of the railway, he had set up his son, Frederick, in a second shop in Station Road. By 1929, in retirement, he was living at St Elmo, Marsham Way.

Servants

Before the arrival of the railway, partly because of the number of servants in the great houses, there were far fewer males in the population than females. This feature became even more marked in the period 1911-31. Three possible explanations exist: the number of servants, the number of widows or spinsters, and the absence of males, particularly, perhaps boys, at boarding school. Of these the last is the least likely, as the census dates were generally in school holidays. If it is assumed that the proportion of males in Gerrards Cross should have been the same as the county average, it is possible to estimate how many extra females there were in Gerrards Cross than in the 'normal' population. In 1901 the figure was 53 and in that year there were 59 domestic servants in the parish. Given that 218 new houses were built between 1901 and 1911, the 290 extra females found in 1911 gives an average of 1.3 per household. If all these were servants, it would mean that on average each household had one live-in servant. Since some households kept several servants, it follows that not all the new houses had servants, despite the fact that so many were built with servants' quarters. In 1921 the ratio had fallen to 1.0 per household, in 1931 to 0.9, and by 1951 to 0.5 per household.

There were local servant recruiting agencies, such as Mrs Hope's Registry for Servants in Oak End Way. The lonely life of a servant in a suburb was to some extent offset by the 'girls club', run by Miss Pitt from Orchehill Chambers. The servant problem was reflected in the frequency with which residents resorted to adverts for new staff in *The Times*, and it may have been that many servants did not like the suburban lifestyle. In 1916, Rose Fisher, then employed at Sevenoaks, Vicarage Way, was advertising for a position as a good plain cook and noted 'town preferred where other maid kept'. The importance of servants can be seen in a 1910 advertisement for Tresco, Marsham Way, which was offered to let 'with servants if desired'. The difficulty of attracting staff may be seen in a 1916 advertisement from Mrs Quartermaine of Katerina, Bulstrode Way, who was seeking a cook general to undertake plain cooking for a family of two, and was offering 'good outings' as well as 'wages according to experience with rise', in a house which already had weekly help. Part of the problem of recruiting servants to such households, even by 1914, was the resistance to going into service as a sole servant. Those who kept more than one servant were careful to note this in their advertisements. Thus in 1916, Mrs Berry of Granville, Vicarage Way, later Lady Kemsley, advertised for a house parlourmaid, noting that she kept a cook general, a between-maid and two nurses for her family of three with two children. In May 1919 she was again advertising for two lady nurses for twin babies, even though she kept an under nurse. Incidentally the advert noted that a house was kept in Swansea until September (presumably on the Gower).

Some of the houses were built with special facilities for servants. Thus Uplands, a five-bedroom house in Marsham Way, included a 'housemaids sink to hot and cold supplies' as well as a butler's pantry, a servants' WC and 'shut off' (a trader's lobby). This house had, however, been designed 'to minimise domestic labour'. This must have been true for most houses built after the war, so some of the trends in middle-class domestic arrangements which were to become common between the wars were quickly apparent in Gerrards Cross. It is likely that most houses kept no more than one servant. Thus, in 1918, an advertisement stated that a superior maid was wanted for Ardsley, Orchehill Avenue, with wages £32-5, to share the mistress work of a small house. There were, however, still families who kept a full establishment of servants. Professor Buxton's wife advertised for servants in 1936: 'Young cook required: kitchenmaid taking first place or single handed might suit; four servants kept; nursery and older children during holidays'. It is not known whether any local mistress took up Harrods' 1930 offer by dressing their servants to suit the architectural style of the house, with 'a choice of Tudor, Cromwellian, Queen Anne/Georgian or Stuart cap and apron styles'.[5]

The lifestyle of the new residents can sometimes be glimpsed from the building regulations plans. Most of the larger four-bedroomed houses had an attic room for a servant, usually with a dormer window facing the rear garden. In 1919, Col Tucker thought it desirable to add a butler's pantry and lavatory to Littlehaye, Bulstrode Way. In 1909, J.W. Western was adding a gardener's cottage to Dinthill, Vicarage Way. Even in 1923, Miss Du Pre was adding such a facility to a house in North Park.

Motor Cars

Nationally motor cars and motor cycles were uncommon in 1906. At Gerrards Cross there were only 11 registered vehicles by June 1905[6] and only four of these were cars. Two were owned by contractors, including one in the name of Paulings, the railway contractors. Col Le Poer Trench owned a steam car, and at Woodbank a car and a motorcycle were registered to a Mr T. Smith. Three of the motorcycles were owned by the sons of the paper merchant, Matthew Roe, at Latchmoor Cottage. The Duke's agent and William Payne, the cycle maker, were others with motorcycles. This early part of the motor age was to cause developers problems: should they provide a stable or a garage?

Even after 1906, some of the new households were still using horses, and not only for leisure. In 1908, a new stable was added to Ravenscroft, Bulstrode Way. Stables were built in 1909 at Jonesboro, and in 1912 at The Turret House, both in Packhorse Road. In 1913 Badminton House also acquired a new stable. The first separate plan for a garage was submitted in 1910 for a house in North Park. Others quickly followed, although they were variously termed 'motor garage', 'motor house', and 'motor shed'.

Advertisements for houses made great play of their being fully fitted and heated.

In the early days of motoring, the dust created by the new form of transport was a significant issue, as was the speed of the vehicles. Even before 1914, the Parish Council called on the County Council to introduce speed limits on the Oxford Road, especially near the junction with the Windsor Road. Later, the Parish Council, along with various county and district councils, lobbied the Minister of Transport for improvements. In 1927 Rees Jeffreys, in a lengthy article in *The Times*, cited the completion of Western Avenue from Wood Lane to Gerrards Cross as one of the five most urgent road schemes in the London area.[7] The road had started in 1920 but took over a decade to complete. In Gerrards Cross, its most notable creation was the backwater that the old road between Woodhill and Coorheen became when the new wider carriageway was created. AA reports of the period constantly emphasise the poor condition of the road. In 1920, it was noted that the road was in bad condition from Gerrards Cross to a mile west of Beaconsfield, but it did have direct effects on life there, such as the existence of two tea rooms in the 1920s, as well as a garage.

A Stable Residential Suburb?

Most of the houses built before 1906 were rented. Not surprisingly there was a considerable turnover of tenants in these properties. In the period 1906–40 this may have reflected an aging tenant base as well as the run down of the great estates. On the Bulstrode estate, at least, rents seem not to have been increased much in the first years after 1906, so there was no pressure on old tenants to move out.

Many of the new houses may have been initially rented, reflecting the situation that was common in England at the time. For developers who were building speculatively and with, from time to time, an excess number of completions, a rent was better than a vacancy. Even after an initial sale, a property may have been rented out by an owner sent on a lengthy overseas posting. The First World War added to the disruptions of family life. The lively rental market conceals the degree to which newcomers found the new Gerrards Cross to their satisfaction. All that can be now calculated is the length of stay in Gerrards Cross of each family, a crude measure as it would ultimately be influenced by deaths.

Tracking the addresses of residents reveals a number of relocations. These may indicate an initial renting whilst a new house was being built, a local presence during the building process being a useful way to control the workmen. A few newcomers even 'down-sized' in the early years. A few had larger houses built as their prosperity rose. The editor of the 1921 local directory was aware of change in Gerrards Cross when he commented that, since the 1917 edition, 'nearly 250 residents had been replaced by others'.

Some examples of such change have been calculated. At Austenway, of the 11 residents listed in 1911, 82 per cent were still there in 1915, 73 per cent in 1917, but none by 1929. Of those new in 1915, 86 per cent were still in residence in 1921, but only 43 per cent in 1929. The effect of the war was considerable. Of those arriving in 1917 none were still in residence by 1929, and most may have left by 1924. Similar rates of change were found in Bulstrode Way. Of the 1911 residents, only 62 per cent remained by 1915, and 23 per cent by 1929. 79 per cent of the new residents in 1915 remained by 1921, but only 29 per cent by 1929. Only seven per cent of the later wartime arrivals of 1917 remained by 1931.

Eight
The End of the Geographical Expansion

The sale and laying out for development of the Bulstrode land largely ended the territorial expansion of the residential areas of Gerrards Cross. After 1945 most new housing was built in the areas already laid out or by infilling elsewhere, including the creation of various cul-de-sacs in order to gain access to back land. The main reason for this has been planning constraints which started in the 1930s. Indeed, the 1932 Bulstrode sale in some ways became part of a wider campaign that led to the creation of Green Belts. In December 1935, *The Times* published a large picture of Bulstrode Park following the launch of a campaign by the Penn Country branch of the CPRE to save some of the Park from development. In 1933 Raymond Unwin, technical advisor to the Greater London Regional Planning Committee, proposed a narrow 'green girdle' around London, designed to compensate for lack of open space for recreation within the city, rather than to halt urban sprawl. As a result a London Green Belt was proposed in 1935. The 1935 Restriction of Ribbon Development Act also crowned CPRE's nine-year campaign against the sprawl of towns and cities across the countryside by inhibiting the long rows of building along main roads leading out of towns.

The Penn branch's letter to *The Times* pointed out that 'the quiet restful beauty of Bulstrode has been inviolate for a thousand years. Now it seems, unless an appeal to preserve a mere hundred acres out of its former 2,000 acres is successful, its beauty will be lost for all time.'

It then stated that the present owner, who had bought the land for development, had apparently consented not to sell for the time being for building purposes and would offer land adjoining the Oxford Road as an open space. 112 acres had been granted on option at a price not exceeding £200 per acre. It was reported that the owner had already received offers to purchase for gravel and sand working and building operations at a higher price than asked in the option (all of which makes the price achieved in 1932 seem very low, or did the owner believe that £200 per acre would not have been too bad a profit to realise?). But in 1937 it was reported that Sir John had re-purchased part of the Bulstrode Park estate, and had offered to sterilise an area near the London-Oxford road, including the whole of the West plantation. This offer was accepted by the County Council.[1]

Mrs Le Poer Trench had the development of the St Hubert's estate in mind, too. In 1936 she proposed to divide the land between the Uxbridge Road and the Fulmer Road into building plots. The plan remained on file at Eton RDC but was never progressed. It is not clear whether the proposal was dropped because of official objections, or lack of demand. Given the slow pace of development on the Bulstrode estate, 1936 was clearly not a good time to be proposing the release of a further large area of development land.

In 1938, an application was made for consent to the development of 500 acres of the Chalfont

Park estate. The County Council decided to ask local councils to refuse the application and negotiations were opened for the acquisition of the land. In 1939 the County Council purchased the Isle of Wight Farm in order to sterilise its land from development. It is likely that assistance was obtained in this purchase from the London County Council who, under the 1938 Green Belt (London and Home Counties) Act, could allocate £2 million to assist local authorities in the purchase of open spaces and pay up to 50 per cent of the cost of any land selected for the Green Belt.

There was another factor in the end of geographical expansion. In the 1930s, as Gerrards Cross spread south, demand for houses as expressed in land prices seems to have fallen. In part this was due to the increasing distance of new sites from the station. What had originally been a railway-linked outpost of Central London was turning into something different. The motor car, providing links to workplaces as varied as Slough, Uxbridge, Pinehurst and Park Royal, as well as Central London, was beginning to free the upper middle classes from the railway's umbilical cord.

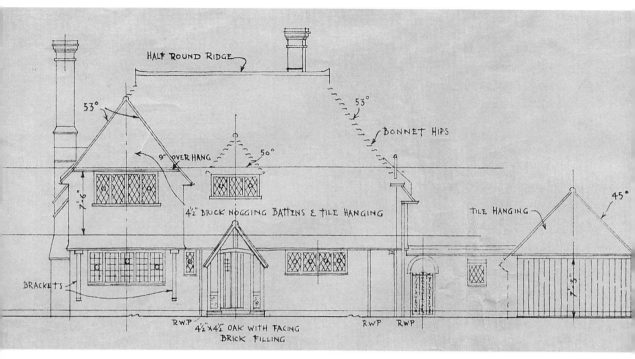

110 Old Tyles, Camp Road, designed by A.L. Abbott, 1936.

FRONT ELEVATION

111 Thorn House, 14 The Woodlands, built in 1908. Alterations and additions by J. Stanley Beard, 1930.

Appendix One
Architects

Several of the architects who set the style of Gerrards Cross from 1906 onwards were from well-known London firms, like Forbes & Tate and Kemp & How, who may have had informal relationships with the builders and developers working on site. Some, like Arnold Mitchell and Baillie Scott, received single, if significant commissions. Others, like Percy Hopkins, John Graham Johnson, Sydney Prevost, Edgar Ranger, Stanley Beard and Robert Muir, actually came to live in Gerrards Cross and made a much greater contribution to the growth of the settlement. The architects who received multiple commissions in Gerrards Cross are listed here in alphabetical order.

Abbott, Albert Leigh
(Queen Anne's Gate, London)
Abbott was born in 1890. He worked for various local authorities in the construction of over 1,000 council houses. He later became a popular exponent of 'stock-broker tudor' architecture, designing over 400 individual homes, restorations and alterations, with contract values ranging from £2,000 to £30,000. His earliest work in Gerrards Cross is Nexdaw, now known as Chiltern House, 34 Orchehill Avenue, built in 1922 for S.L. Townsend-Greene. He later went into partnership with Douglas Tanner, who probably introduced him to Y.J. Lovell & Son. The partners were heavily involved in the Ideal Home Exhibition designs in the 1930s. Abbott designed at least four of the Lovell houses on the Woodhill estate, the best being The Bumbles,

8 Woodhill Avenue, built in 1935. He designed Olde Tyles, 22 Camp Road, in 1936. Abbott also designed factories and research laboratories and worked for the Ministry of Aircraft Production and the War Office. After the Second World War he was involved in several London County Council housing schemes.

Banfield, Ernest W.
(Queen Victoria Street, London)
Ernest W. Banfield was born in 1873, the son of William Banfield, a London accountant. In 1906, he worked for George Hampton, designing two pairs of semi-detached houses in Marsham Way. In 1909, he designed Tresco, now Grove House, 23 Marsham Way, and Highcroft, now Merrydown, 51 Marsham Way. He also designed Redcliffe, later known as Mill Corner, 60 Marsham Way, for Miss S. Jarrett in 1913. He was employed in 1920 on alterations and additions to Redcliffe for E.H. Burgess. Banfield designed the first block of flats for the St Marylebone Housing Association in 1928.

Beard, John Stanley
(Baker Street, London)
Beard was the founder and for many years senior partner in the firm of Beard, Bennett, Wilkins & Partners. He specialised in the design of theatres, music halls and cinemas, and designed the Gerrards Cross Picture Playhouse in 1925. He lived at The Barn House, Oak End Way, and later at Bearwood, South Park, both of which have been demolished. Perhaps his

112   Mill End, 21 Mill Lane, designed by J. Stanley Beard, 1915.

best work in Gerrards Cross was the design of Mill End, 21 Mill Lane, for Capt. W. Carey, in 1915. J. Stanley Beard also designed the shops on Packhorse Road originally known as The Highway, including W.H. Smith and Boots the Chemists. He retired to Dorset in 1950 where he restored the gardens at Compton Acres, Poole. He died there in 1970.

Boddy, Percy Charles (Ruislip)

Percy Charles Boddy was born in London in 1881, although his father was from Beaconsfield.

His first independent practice was in Ruislip, Middlesex. In 1908 he formed a partnership with J. Graham Johnson, who already had offices at Station Approach, Gerrards Cross, and at Beaconsfield. They also had offices at 14 Southampton Square, Strand. It seems likely that it was Johnson, rather than Boddy, who prepared the drawings for the 50 Gerrards Cross houses designed by the partnership during the years 1908-12. When Johnson left the firm in 1912, he was replaced at Gerrards Cross by Charles Davis. The seven Davis & Boddy

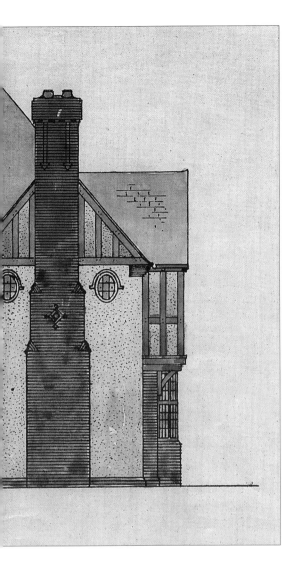

building applications in 1912-13 are in a very different style. After H.P. Green joined the partnership in 1913, the firm made a further four applications as Davis, Boddy & Green during 1913-14.

When Percy Boddy applied for Fellowship of the Royal Institute of British Architects in 1925, his list of architectural works included houses at Beaconsfield, Fulmer and Gerrards Cross, and a school in Gerrards Cross. Many of these buildings were in fact designed by J. Graham Johnson and Charles Davis. Percy Charles Boddy

lived in Ruislip and is particularly known for his designs on the Grange Estate, Northwood. He died on 1 January 1964.

Burgess, Julian Gulson (Burke's Parade, Beaconsfield)

Burgess was born in Leicester in 1876 and educated at Rugby. He was articled to his uncle, Edward Burgess, architect, of Gray's Inn, London, but moved to Beaconsfield about the time of the opening of the new railway line to London. In 1906, he joined a partnership with the local surveyor, Legender W. Myers, who was also engaged on surveying the Gregories estate for James and William Gurney, and Leonard P. Kerkham, an architect working on the Gurney's Orchehill estate at Gerrards Cross. The firm was known as Kerkham, Burgess & Myers, and designed over thirty houses on the Orchehill and Latchmoor estates, as well as the fine row of shops on the corner of Packhorse Road and Oak End Way. A good example of their domestic architecture is The Rowans, 22 Marsham Way, which was designed in 1907 for John Bailey, the builder. Kerkham, Burgess & Myers' offices were in Orchehill Chambers, Packhorse Road, also designed by the firm. When Kerkham left the partnership by mutual consent in 1908, Burgess & Myers concentrated on their work in Beaconsfield. Their distinctive offices, above Lloyds Bank in Burke's Parade, Beaconsfield, are the best local example of commercial architecture in the Edwardian period. Julian Burgess built his own house, Netherlands, at Penn Road, Knotty Green, about 1907. It is a small Arts and Crafts house with unusual Dutch gables.

When Legender W. Myers joined the Ford Motor Company in 1914, Walter Holden, who had been with the firm since 1907, was made a partner. The gap left by Myers in the surveying area was filled by C.H. Watson. Burgess, Holden and Watson took on several council housing schemes for Eton Rural District and

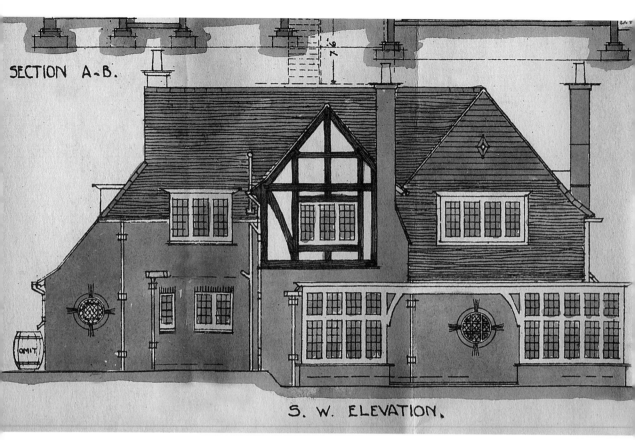

SECTION A-B.

S. W. ELEVATION.

113 Diss Park, Marsham Lane, designed by Kerkham, Burgess & Myers for James Gurney, 1906.

Beaconsfield Urban District Councils. Julian Burgess was the architect for the Church of England Schools at Beaconsfield and designed several branch premises for Lloyds Bank, in particular that at Watford. He became an FRIBA in 1925, and died at Netherlands on 4 May 1933.

Davis, Charles

Davis was active in Beaconsfield and Gerrards Cross from 1910 and had offices at 1 Station Parade, Beaconsfield, and at 59 Pennards Road, Shepherds Bush. He designed The Brambles, 14 Orchehill Avenue, Woolton House, 4 Oval Way, and Glendruid, 10 Oval Way, all in 1911, and Mill Lane Lodge, 41 Mill Lane, in 1912. In 1913, he replaced J. Graham Johnson in the firm of Johnson & Boddy, which now became Davis

& Boddy and, briefly, Davis, Boddy & Green. His 1913 drawings of Farleigh, 56 Bulstrode Way, and Fencourt, 6 Oval Way, both for Davis & Boddy, are so similar in style and graphics to his earlier independent work that it is obvious that he was the active partner in the firm's Gerrards Cross operation. Davis & Boddy made seven Gerrards Cross building applications from 1912-13, and a further four application as Davis, Boddy & Green during 1913-14. These included the extensions to Gerrards Cross Church of England School in 1913, and Heathside, 12 Fulmer Way, in 1914.

Eves, William Lionel (Uxbridge)

Eves succeeded his father as surveyor to Uxbridge Urban District Council, and was the architect for several of Uxbridge's housing

NORTH ELEVATION

114 The Rowans. 22 Marsham Way, designed by Kerkham, Burgess & Myers, 1907.

115 Glendruid, 10 Oval Way, designed by Charles Davis for George Welch, 1911.

116   Farleigh, 56 Bulstrode Way, designed by Davis & Boddy, 1913.

117   Allendale, 53 Bulstrode Way, designed by Fair & Myer, 1908, with alterations by Arthur May, 1934.

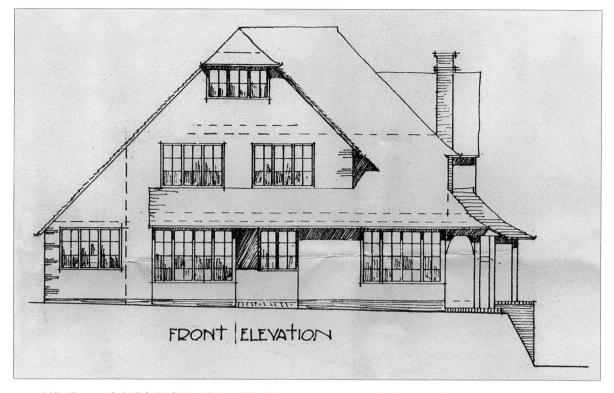

118 Eastwood, 9 Oak End Way, designed by Fair & Myer, 1908, with alterations by R.G. Muir, 1920.

schemes. He was, therefore, well known to the Uxbridge builders who developed land in Gerrards Cross. He designed the semi-detached houses built in Bulstrode Way and Marsham Way by A.H. James of Uxbridge. He also designed Chalfont End, 42 North Park and the extension to Woodbank for Sam Fay. He continued in practice at High Street, Uxbridge until his death in 1950.

Fair & Myer
(London and Henley-on-Thames)
John William Fair was born in 1871. From 1905 to 1914 he was in partnership with George Val Myer. The firm were appointed consulting architects for Woldsea Garden City, Lincolnshire, in 1911. Notable Gerrards Cross houses by Fair & Myer include The Haven, 45 Bulstrode Way, built in 1907; Holmbury, 28 Bulstrode Way; Blewbury House, 51 Bulstrode Way; and Allendale, 53 Bulstrode Way, all built in 1908; Eastwood, 9 Oak End Way, also built in 1908, and Cranford, Layters Way, built in 1909. J.W. Fair died in 1915.

Forbes & Tate
(Grosvenor Square, London)
James Edwin Forbes was born in 1876. He was in partnership with John Duncan Tate from 1905 to 1930, when their work appeared regularly in the architectural press. The firm is best known for Pollards Park House, Chalfont St Giles, 1907, and Pednor House, Chesham, 1911. At Gerrards Cross, they designed several houses in Oval Way for Harold Raffety, including The Pollards, Brown Cottage and Kimberley. They also designed The Paddock House and Widenham House on West Common.

Hamp, Stanley Hinge
(Bloomsbury Square, London)
Hamp was born in 1877. He was in partnership with Thomas Edward Collcutt, architect of the

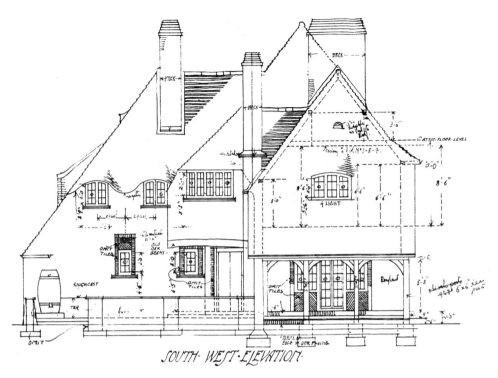

119   The Pollards, 3 Oval Way, designed by Forbes & Tate for Harold Raffety, 1907.

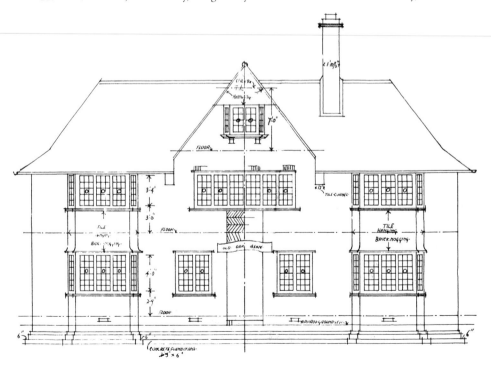

120   Kimberley, 22 Oval Way, designed by Forbes & Tate, 1908.

Savoy Hotel and President of the Royal Institute of British Architects from 1904 until his death in 1924. Stanley Hamp himself was president of the Architectural Association in 1922 and a Vice President of the RIBA from 1935 to 1937. In 1941 he served on the committee set up to plan the future of the RIBA after the war.

Hamp's original contribution to the architectural development of Gerrards Cross was the adaptation of Marsham Farm (now called Marsham Manor), Marsham Lane, in 1907 for Selby Lowndes. In the same year he designed Abbotsmead, also in Marsham Lane. Stanley Hamp also designed several houses in Beaconsfield, including Davenies Barn, which featured in the *Studio Yearbook of Decorative Art* in 1921. Stanley Hamp is perhaps best known for the starkly modern flat-roofed houses he designed for sites in Windsor Road, Gerrards Cross, and Cambridge Road, Beaconsfield, in the 1930s. One of these white cement-rendered houses appeared in *Architecture Illustrated* in September 1934. Stanley Hamp died in 1968 at the age of 91.

Hooper, Frederick Billett (Easton Street, High Wycombe)

Hooper was born in 1881. He was one of the first local architects to see the opportunity afforded by the opening of the railway to Gerrards Cross and Beaconsfield. In 1906, his firm, Hooper & Nash, built a house and office in Bulstrode Way, near to its junction with Packhorse Road. Hooper & Nash also bought the neighbouring plot, where they built a rather old-fashioned house later known as Ingleside, 2 Bulstrode Way. Hooper & Nash did not prosper in Gerrards Cross, although they did build several houses in Chalfont St Peter and in Penn.

121 Abbotsmead, 5 Marsham Lane, designed by Collcutt & Hamp, 1907.

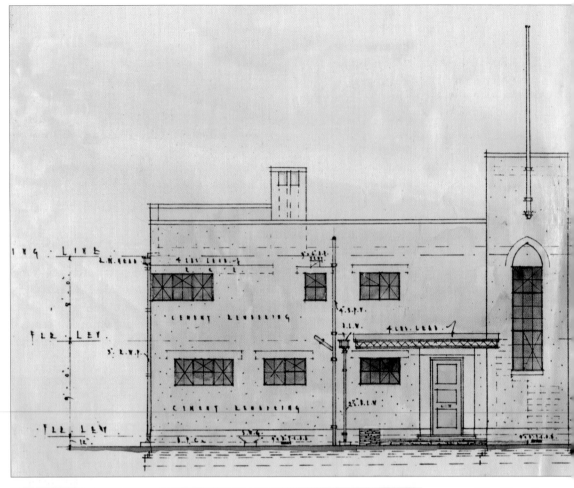

122 Kings Lea, 101 Windsor Road, designed by Stanley Hamp, 1934.

123 Whitewood, Windsor Road, now demolished, designed by Stanley Hamp, 1934.

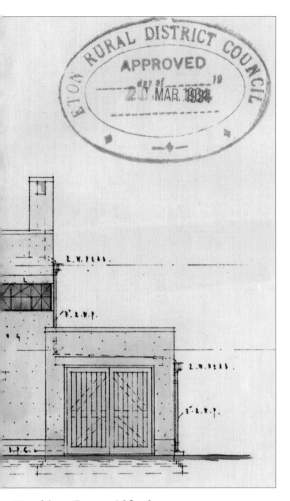

124 St Bernards, 90 Oak End Way, designed by P. Morley Horder, 1906.

Hopkins, Percy Alfred

Hopkins was born in London in 1873, the son of Alfred James Hopkins, architect, of Brooklyn Road, Hammersmith. By 1901 he was an architect's assistant in London. A member of the Society of Architects, he was quick to see the potential of housing developments next to the newly opened railway lines to London. He moved to Gerrards Cross about 1906, where he had offices in Station Approach and later at Oak End Way. He also had offices at Amersham, Beaconsfield and 37 Mortimer Street, London. Hopkins was in partnership first with J. Graham Johnson in 1907, and with W.J. Walker in 1908, working on the Milton Park estate. One of his designs, Churston, Bull Lane, featured in

an advertisement for the estate in the 1908 edition of *Where to Live Round London*. He bought land in Oak End Way on which he built an inelegant row of six half-timbered shops in 1907. He put up an equally modest row of eight cottages in Marsham Lane in 1912. He also designed the Assembly Room, Oak End Way, 1913, for the Oak End Estate Ltd, of which he was probably the leading shareholder. During the First World War, Percy Hopkins was a Major and, later, a Lieutenant Colonel in the London Regiment. He returned to Gerrards Cross after the war and lived at Cressings, School Lane, Chalfont St Peter. He was elected to the RIBA Council and was the Honorary Treasurer in 1935.

Horder, Percy Richard Morley
(New Bond Street, London)

P. Morley Horder was born in 1870. His work regularly appeared in the architectural press in the early 1900s. He designed two houses in Gerrards Cross: St Bernards, 90 Oak End Way, was built in a very modern style for H. Prescot Mosley in 1906 and was later the home of E.L. Colston, joint managing director of the Hoover Company; the other house was Oldhurst, 35 Bulstrode Way, built for Edward Rouse in 1909 in the English Cottage style. The

125   Oldhurst, 35 Bulstrode Way, designed by P. Morley Horder, 1909.

frontage to Bulstrode Way is particularly fine in its composition. Horder died in 1944.

Johnson, John Graham

Johnson was born in London on 26 January 1882. He obtained his architectural training in London in the 1890s, first as an articled pupil for three years to Charles Forster Hayward, and then as improver for two years and assistant for two more years to J.E.K. & J.P. Cutts. In 1907 he worked with Percy Hopkins at Gerrards Cross and Beaconsfield, designing eight houses in Gerrards Cross. During 1908 he worked independently, designing a further eight houses in Gerrards Cross, including South Park House, 8 South Park Drive, for Y.J. Lovell & Son.

At the end of 1908, J. Graham Johnson began a fruitful partnership with Percy Charles Boddy of Ruislip. As there is no perceptible change in the style and lettering of the drawings produced before and after the formation of this partnership, it seems likely that Johnson managed the Gerrards Cross business from his office at Station Approach, whilst Boddy continued to work on commissions in the Ruislip area. J. Graham Johnson was the most prolific of the Gerrards Cross architects, designing over fifty houses during his two-year partnership with Percy Charles Boddy. Johnson was the master of the façade, using different elements of cottage architecture to give each four-bedroom house a different appearance. His design for Noris (now Lynbury), 14 South Park Crescent, featured in Y.J. Lovell's advertisement in *Where to Live Around London*, in 1910. At this time, J. Graham Johnson was living at Merton, Marsham Way, Gerrards Cross.

J. Graham Johnson dissolved his partnership with Percy Charles Boddy in 1912 and moved to Victoria, British Columbia. After service during the First World War, he returned to Canada, and was in private practice at Kentville, Nova Scotia, for five years. For health reasons Johnson returned to Victoria, becoming Resident Architect for the Canadian Pacific Railway. In 1930, he resigned to establish his private practice in Victoria. There he designed many houses, particularly in Oak Bay, sometimes using the Arts and Crafts style, but he was equally

126 L'Abri (now known as Doulma), 11 Fulmer Way, was built by C.C. Baldwin in 1909 to the design of Johnson & Boddy.

comfortable employing the Modern style. He died in Victoria, 27 July 1945, aged 63.

Kemp & How
(Bloomsbury Square, London)

William James Kemp was born in 1882, the son of W.J. Kemp FRIBA (1853-1926). In 1905, he formed a partnership with William Murthwaite How (1873-1957), son of Frederick How, solicitor, Chesham. They designed extensions to Dr Challoner's Grammar School, Amersham, in 1910, alterations and a new vestry at Chesham Bois church in 1911, and the new Post Office, Gerrards Cross, in 1912. Their best work in Gerrards Cross is The Old Tile House, 2 Layters Way, built in 1910.

Kerkham, Leonard Percy

Kerkham was born in King's Lynn, Norfolk in 1868. He practised as an architect at Harrow, before moving to Gerrards Cross about 1905. He formed a partnership with a local surveyor, Legender William Myers (1879-1958), and designed several of the early houses at the northern end of the Orchehill estate. When he was joined in the partnership by Julian Burgess, the firm produced designs for over thirty houses on the Orchehill and Latchmoor estates. In 1908, Leonard Kerkham withdrew from the firm by mutual consent and continued in independent practice at Gerrards Cross, with offices above the London

— Front Elevation: —

127   Old Tile House, 2 Layters Way, designed by Kemp & How, 1910.

& South Western Bank. He lived at Horning, Austenwood, but later moved to West Byfleet, Surrey. In the period 1908-15, he designed a further 16 houses, mostly at Kingsway and The Firs Estate, Austenwood Common. He favoured half-hipped gables and bay windows with flat roofs. One of his architectural signatures was to leave four bricks or tiles protruding from the white pebble-dash white walls, in the shape of a diamond. One of Kerkham's most unusual buildings was Thorpe House School, Oval Way, designed for George Burgoyne in 1925.

Muir, Robert George

Muir was born in 1890. As a partner in Wood, Sarvis and Muir, 17 Hard Street, London, he worked on several major contracts in Gerrards Cross. The firm designed two very large houses in Bull Lane in 1910, Hayes Barton for Major Amesbury, and Bull Mead for Thomas Wordley. Wood Sarvis & Muir also designed Badminton House, Marsham Way, for W.E. Preston. Robert Muir became an ARIBA in 1912 and was an FRIBA by 1924. In independent practice, he had offices at 1 Raymond Buildings, Grays Inn, London, and a small office at the back of

128 9 Latchmoor Avenue, designed by Leonard P. Kerkham for George Burgoyne, 1925.

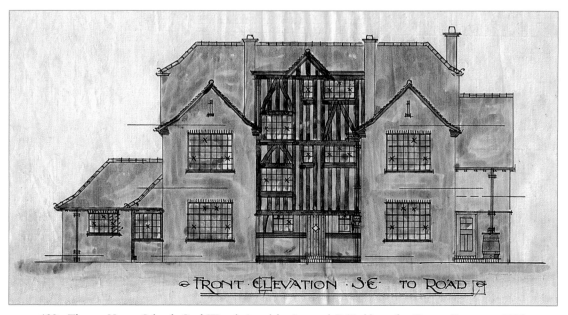

129 Thorpe House School, Oval Way, designed by Leonard P. Kerkham for George Burgoyne, 1925.

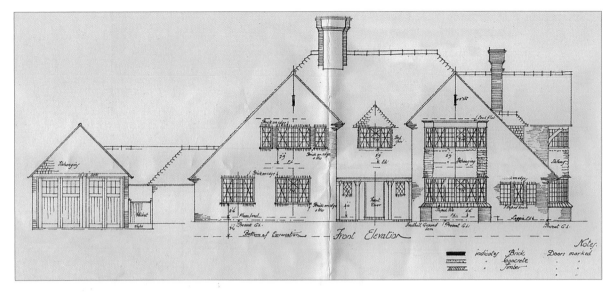

130   Arkley, 69 Marsham Way, designed by Robert G. Muir in 1922.

Augustus Gibbons, estate agents, Station Parade, Gerrards Cross. He laid out the new roads on the Ethorpe estate in 1923, and designed several of the houses there, as well as alterations and additions to the hotel itself. Muir's own house, Broadeaves, Ethorpe Close, featured in *The Builder* in 1930. His houses resemble those of Edgar Ranger, with liberal use of tile-hanging to soften the appearance. His most elegant houses are Arkley, 69 Marsham Way, and Southwood, 26 South Park, both built in 1922. Three of his houses are in close proximity in Orchehill Avenue: 1 Orchehill Avenue was built in 1920; Cary House (now Rampos Edge), 19 Orchehill Avenue, was built in 1924; and the present Carey House, 21 Orchehill Avenue, was built for Miss Audrey Baker, about 1960. He also designed the new *French Horn Inn* in 1946. At his death in 1968, Robert G. Muir left £145,149 gross.

Myers, Legender William

Legender W. Myers was born in London in 1878, but he was brought up in Beaconsfield where his mother was a lace dealer. He was articled to Arthur Vernon, architect and surveyor, High Wycombe, and later worked in architects and surveyors offices in Cambridge. He returned to Beaconsfield in 1905 when he was engaged by James and William Gurney to lay out the Orchehill estate at Gerrards Cross and the Gregories estate at Beaconsfield. He formed a partnership first with Leonard P. Kerkham, architect, at Gerrards Cross, and then with Julian Burgess, who was based in Beaconsfield. Legender W. Myers left Burgess & Myers in 1914 when he joined the Ford Motor Company. He worked with Kennard & Kennard in laying out the Woodhill estate in 1923 and died in 1958.

Prevost, Sydney James

Prevost was born in 1870, the son of a London publican. A partner in J.C. Richards & Co., builders, in Paddington, he moved to Gerrards Cross in 1906. He acted as the surveyor for the London & Country Investment & Property Company in the development of the Latchmoor estate. Two of his designs, West Lodge, 48 Bulstrode Way, and Briarhedge, 33 Orchehill Avenue, featured in *Live in the Country*, 1910. He also designed Crosfield House, South Park

131 Broadeaves, Ethorpe Close, designed by Robert G. Muir, 1930.

132 The *French Horn*, Oxford Road, designed by Robert G. Muir in 1946.

133 Architect's impression of West Lodge, 48 Bulstrode Way, designed by Sydney Prevost and built in 1908 by the London & Country Investment & Property Company.

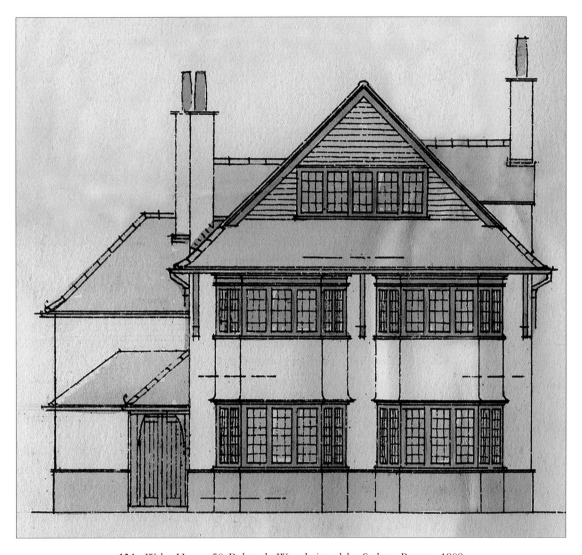

134   Wyke House, 50 Bulstrode Way, designed by Sydney Prevost, 1908.

(now demolished), and four of the large houses in Vicarage Way. He lived at La Moye (now Orient), 80 Packhorse Road, before taking the same house name to 48 Bulstrode Way. Sydney James Prevost served as a Gerrards Cross representative on Eton Rural District Council. He died in London, 14 February 1944.

Ranger, Edgar
Ranger was born at East Peckham, near Tunbridge Wells, in 1888, and educated at

Bradfield College, Berkshire. In training to become an architect, he made a particular study of the domestic architecture of Kent and Surrey. From 1906 to 1909 he was articled to the firm of Kerkham, Burgess & Myers, architects, Gerrards Cross, and he may well have worked on large houses such as Diss Park, Marsham Lane. Ranger set up an independent practice in Gerrards Cross, in 1911, with offices in Orchehill Chambers, Station Parade. Developing a large plot of land to the north of Austenwood

135 Wisteria Cottage, 53 Orchehill Avenue, designed by Sydney Prevost, 1912.

136 Kinnerton (now Craiglea House), Austenwood Lane, designed by Edgar Ranger, featured in the *Studio Yearbook of Decorative Art*, 1914.

Common, he built The Downs and Kinnerton (now Craiglea House), in 1911, and his own house, Old Basing, in 1912. He used the same patterns of half-timbering and tile-hanging he had observed in the cottages of southern England. He was to build two more houses nearby, Kaduna in 1915, and Cottered in 1919. Ranger served in the Army during the First World War and afterwards set up a practice in Broadstairs and at Gray's Inn Square, London. He was made a FRIBA in 1931. His most notable Buckinghamshire house is Spinfields, Marlow, built in 1936. He died in 1971.

Tanner, Douglas George (1880-1932)

Tanner was born in 1880. He was articled to Chancellor & Hill, architects, Winchester, before setting up in private practice at Eastbourne in 1909. He practised in Birmingham in partnership with Arthur L. Horseburgh, 1917-1929. From 1929 until his early death in 1932 he practised in London. Douglas Tanner

developed a close relationship with Y.J. Lovell & Son and designed many of their houses on the Woodhill estate. He designed several of the 'Lovell Homes' which featured in the Ideal Home Exhibitions at Olympia from 1923. Tanner was responsible for the complete design of the Exhibition, 1930-32.

Wood, Kenneth

Wood was born in 1870. He was articled in 1888 to the Sunderland architect Henry Grieves, but later worked as assistant to various architects in London. He started a practice in Byfleet and Woking, Surrey, when wealthy London businessmen were commissioning country houses near the local golf courses. In 1906, Wood formed a partnership with John Sarvis, designing houses in Byfleet, St George's Hill, Weybridge, Hook Heath, Woking, Pyrford, and elsewhere in Surrey. As the market for larger country houses declined, their practice concentrated on smaller houses,

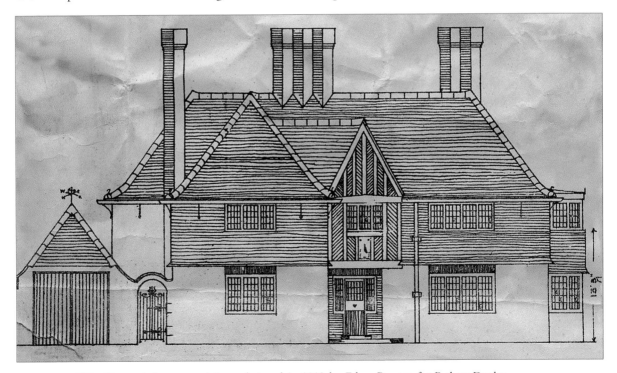

137   Cottered, Austenwood Lane, designed in 1919 by Edgar Ranger for Robert Dredge.

138 Bull Mead, Gerrards Cross, designed by K. Wood, J. Sarvis & R.G. Muir, which featured in the *Studio Yearbook of Decorative Art* in 1916.

business premises, shops, offices, village halls and Wesleyan churches. R.G. Muir, who was a resident of Gerrards Cross, joined the partnership in about 1910. After Sarvis's death in 1928, Kenneth Wood formed a partnership with C.H. Rose, of Leatherhead, Surrey, and continued in practice as Kenneth Wood & Rose, at Woking and Leatherhead, until the Second World War. Wood died at Woking in 1943.

Notable houses in Gerrards Cross by Wood, Sarvis & Muir include Hayes Barton, Bull Lane, built in 1910, Bull Mead, Bull Lane (subsequently known as Carmel and later as Braid House), 1911, and Badminton House, 38 Marsham Way, 1913.

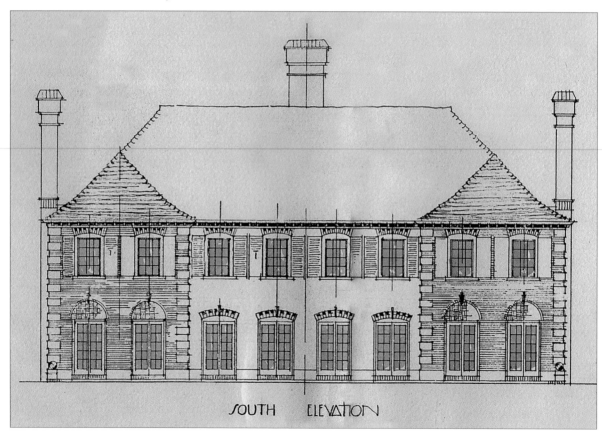

SOUTH ELEVATION

139 Badminton House, 38 Marsham Way, designed by Wood, Sarvis & Muir, 1913.

Appendix Two
Builders

Many of the firms who set up builder's yards in Gerrards Cross after 1906, like J.C. Richards and J.W. Falkner, had been involved in housing development in west London for many years. Firms like Franklin & Fisk of Rickmansworth and Henry Geeves of Uxbridge would regard the development of Gerrards Cross as a natural extension of their work. Some builders, like Henry Brown of Stoke Newington, did come to live in Gerrards Cross, however, and therefore took a more active role in the development of specific areas. C.P. Lovell soon found that his branch yard at Gerrards Cross was more profitable than his father's original business in Marlow. Those firms who built several houses in Gerrards Cross are listed here in alphabetical order.

Bailey, John
(Spencer Road, Wealdstone)

John Bailey & Co. established a builder's yard at the far end and north side of Station Road, Gerrards Cross, in 1907. He soon built The Rowans, 22 Marsham Way, for his own use, and several other large houses, including Swarthmore, Marsham Lane, for Mrs Stevenson in 1910, Bull Mead, Bull Lane, for Thomas Wordley in 1911, and Badminton House, Marsham Way, for William Preston in 1913. Bailey also built the London, County & Westminster Bank in 1912. Bailey's yard in Station Road closed about 1935, but was later occupied by the builders Brown & Langford.

Baldwin, Claude Christopher

Baldwin was brought up in Kensington where his father, Christopher Baldwin, was an architect, surveyor and builder. He moved to Gerrards Cross about 1909 and lived at 2 South View, Bull Lane. He later built himself a new house called Hillcrest, now known as Greystones, Oxford Road, opposite the *Bull Inn*. His builder's yard later became the Oxford Road Garage. During the period 1909-20, Baldwin built six houses in Bulstrode Way, one in Fulmer Way, two in Marsham Way, one in Milton Avenue, two in Oxford Road and one in Vicarage Way. He usually worked in partnership with the surveyor, George Francis Duck, with whom he developed the row of seven shops now numbered 20-34 Packhorse Road. In 1914, the partners purchased part of the grounds of Bull Mead, Bull Lane, which was laid out as an extension to Layters Way. Baldwin built six houses to G.F. Duck's designs in Layters Way during 1914-15. By 1930, Baldwin had moved to Longfield, Shripney, West Sussex.

Brown, Henry
(329 Harrow Road, London)

Brown was born in Hackney in 1850. By 1891 he was in business as a builder at Stoke Newington, but he later moved his premises to Harrow Road. He moved to Gerrards Cross about 1907 and bought several large building plots to the north of Orche Hill House. Here he built large detached houses with particularly heavy half-timbering.

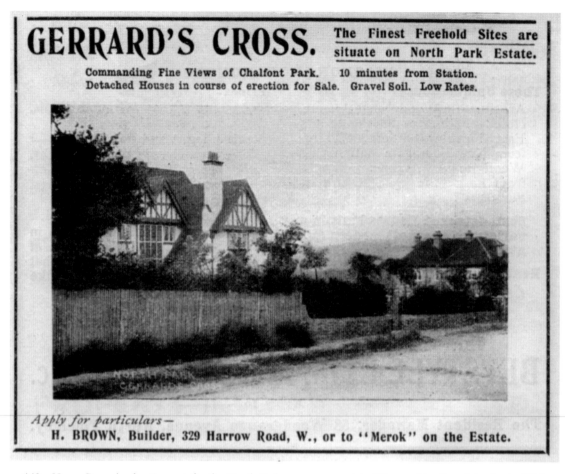

GERRARD'S CROSS.

The Finest Freehold Sites are situate on North Park Estate.

Commanding Fine Views of Chalfont Park.   10 minutes from Station.
Detached Houses in course of erection for Sale.   Gravel Soil.   Low Rates.

Apply for particulars —
H. BROWN, Builder, 329 Harrow Road, W., or to "Merok" on the Estate.

140   Henry Brown's advertisement for the North Park estate appeared in *Where to Live Round London* in 1910.

His own house, Merok (now known as Barton Grange, 28 North Park), features in his advert for the North Park estate in *Where to Live Round London* in 1910. Another of his large half-timbered houses, Riva, 54 North Park, appeared in H.C. Moore's *Gerrards Cross, Beaconsfield and the Chalfonts* in 1910. Henry Brown's greatest contribution to the Gerrards Cross landscape was, however, the fine row of shops on the corner of Station Parade and Oak End Way. These shops were designed by Kerkham, Burgess & Myers for Henry Brown in 1907. About 1917, Brown moved from Merok to another house of his own design and construction, Oakfields, 58 North Park. In 1923 he built a further house, Roughwood, on East Common. He died there

in 1924, but two of his unmarried daughters, Lillian and Florence, continued to live there until 1928. Henry Brown's firm was continued by his son, Harry Stanley Brown, who was still building houses in Denham in 1935. Roughwood has recently been demolished and replaced by a modern house.

Burgess, Ernest Henry (Berners Street, London)

Burgess set up his builder's yard and offices on the south side of Station Road, Gerrards Cross, in 1908. He built one house in Latchmoor Avenue, two in Layters Way and two in Marsham Way. His most notable commission was the building of The Paddock House, West

Common, designed by Forbes & Tate, in 1911. E.H. Burgess built his own house, Oban, now Cleveland, 34 Marsham Way, in 1911. He later moved to Redcliffe, now Mill Corner, 60 Marsham Way, which he extended in 1920. Burgess's yard in Station Road was next to Joseph Nutt's coal yard. It closed about 1935. Burgess died at Epsom on 9 April 1945.

Cocks, H. & Son

At the time of the sale of the Bulstrode estate in 1932, Henry Cocks was renting a builder's yard on the Oxford Road. The firm received commissions for minor repairs and alterations, but does not appear to have built complete houses. Henry Cocks was for many years a member of Gerrards Cross Parish Council.

Falkner, John William & Sons

Falkner & Sons, builders, Ossory Road, Old Kent Road was founded by William John Falkner (1804-64) and continued by his son, John William Falkner (1844-1909). He built the shops in Hill Avenue, Amersham. The firm was carried on by the grandson, Alfred Beech Falkner, who died in 1942. J.W. Falkner and Sons had a builder's yard on the south side of Station Road, Gerrards Cross. They built a house in Layters Way, designed by Kemp & How, and extended Eaglehurst, Orchehill Avenue, for Wills and Kaula. The firm closed its yard in Station Road, Gerrards Cross, in about 1935, but retained their premises off the Old Kent Road until the 1990s.

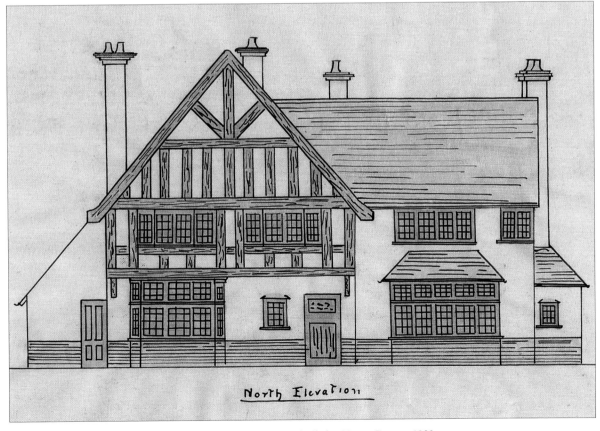

141 Roughwood, East Common, built by Henry Brown, 1923.

142   The Turret House, Packhorse Road, built by Franklin & Fisk in 1908.

Fowler, Albert

In 1903, Albert Fowler built a row of six cottages, called South View, near the new railway bridge on Bull Lane. He lived in one of the cottages, and his partner, Eli Buttle, lived in another. Another house in the row was occupied by Claude Baldwin, who later set up his own building firm. Yet another house in the row was rented by Walter Segrove, a carpenter, whose son, Eric, began as office boy at Y.J. Lovell & Son and rose to be a director of the firm. Albert Fowler dissolved his partnership with Eli Buttle in 1908. His widow was still living in South View in 1933.

Franklin & Fisk
(Rectory Road, Rickmansworth)

Franklin & Fisk bought several plots of land on the west side of Packhorse Road at the sale of the Orchehill estate in 1906. They erected several detached houses on this land, including Turret House. The principal of the firm was Ernest J. Franklin, who lived at South Road, Chorley Wood.

Geeves, Henry (Uxbridge)

Geeves moved to Chalfont St Peter about 1908. He bought several building plots from Hamptons, in Bulstrode Way and Marsham Way. Most of Geeves's houses were designed by John Graham Johnson, including Treetops, 23 Bulstrode Way, and Marsham Cottage, 20 Marsham Way. Henry Geeves went bankrupt in 1910.

Gibbings, Charles E.
(Albany Street, Regents Park, London)

Gibbings established a builder's yard at Beaconsfield about 1907. Between 1907 and

1914 he built houses in Orchehill Avenue, Oval Way and The Woodlands, mostly for the developers Robinson & Roods.

Green, Frank

Green was one of the earliest builders to set up in Gerrards Cross. He lived in Oak End Way and ran his builder's yard next to London House, Station Road. He was a popular choice for building moderately sized houses in Gerrards Cross, receiving several commissions via the architect, Sydney Prevost, and the London & Country Investment & Property Company. He built two houses in Bulstrode Way in 1911, three in Layters Way, 1909-10, four in Orchehill Avenue, 1909-15, two in Oval Way in 1911 and 1915, and four in Vicarage Way, 1912-13. Green's builder's yard remained in Station Road until the 1960s.

Lovell, Y.J. & Son

Lovell's was founded by Young James Lovell (1842-1911), who took over an existing building firm in Marlow in 1876. He built a new wing at Temple House, Bisham, for General Owen Williams and won the contracts for rebuilding Marlow church in 1882 and again in 1890. His son, Clifford Percy Lovell, encouraged him to establish a branch office and builder's yard at Marsham Lane, Gerrards Cross, in 1906 in order to get into the quality housing market. A house called Marlow Cottage was built next to the offices in Marsham Lane for the works manager, William Blake. Y.J. Lovell & Son also had an office at Gerrards Cross Station, from which materials were moved by horse and cart directly to local building sites.

After the death of Young James Lovell, in 1911, the business was carried on by C.P. Lovell, who lived at Belma (now Ben More), Oak End Way. His son, Peter Lovell, also entered the business and lived at Montrose, Marsham Way. The firm built over seventy large detached houses in Gerrards Cross between 1906 and 1920. In 1923, C.P. Lovell purchased part of the Woodhill estate from the executors of Col William Le Poer Trench. The land was divided into 81 building plots, most of which

143 Y.J. Lovell & Son's first offices at Gerrards Cross were built at the junction of Station Road and Marsham Lane in 1906.

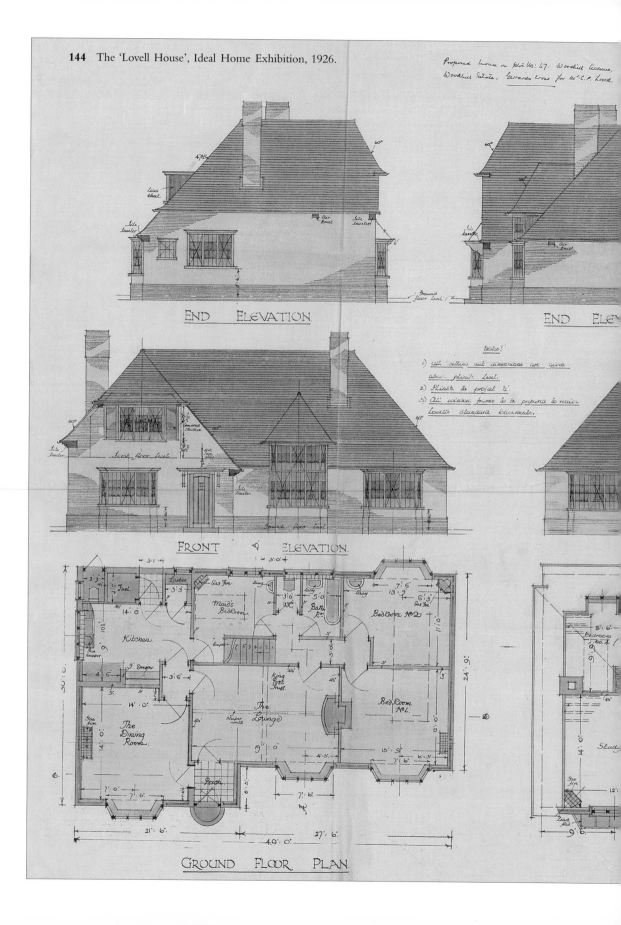

END ELEVATION.

END ELEV

FRONT ELEVATION.

GROUND FLOOR PLAN.

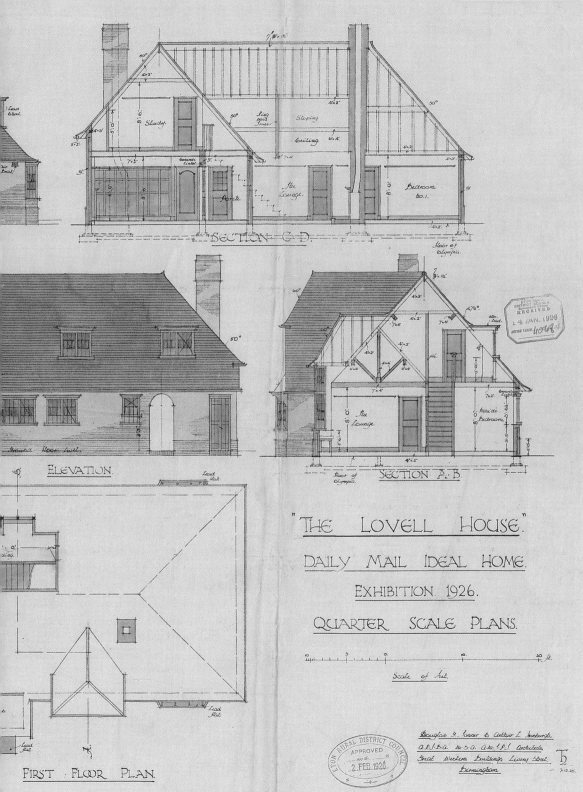

SECTION. C. D.

ELEVATION.

SECTION. A. B.

"THE LOVELL HOUSE"

DAILY MAIL IDEAL HOME.

EXHIBITION. 1926.

QUARTER SCALE PLANS.

Scale of feet.

FIRST FLOOR PLAN.

Douglas G. Harper & Arthur L. Roxburgh,
A.R.I.B.A. to S.A. A.ta. I.P.S. Architects,
Great Western Buildings, Livery Street,
Birmingham.

145 This group of Lovell staff at Gerrards Cross, 26 July 1907, includes from left to right, seated: William Blake, manager, and Frank Barksfield, site supervisor; standing: Blake junior; Brand, Drew and Foster.

were developed speculatively by Y.J. Lovell & Son. Many of the houses were designed by Douglas Tanner and A.L. Abbott, the firm's favoured architects. Each year from 1923-38, a 'Lovell' house featured in the Daily Mail Ideal Home Exhibition. The firm had to erect the house at Olympia in only three weeks. After the three-week run of the exhibition, it had to be demolished and cleared within one week.

Y.J. Lovell & Son was run as a partnership until 1938, when the firm ran into financial difficulties. It was saved by a management buy-out led by Ernest Burrows and Eric Segrove, who bought the business back from the receivers and re-established Y.J. Lovell &

Son as a private limited company. This did not solve C.P. Lovell's own financial problems, which resulted in bankruptcy proceedings in 1940. Although he spent his later years at Bournemouth, Lovell maintained his links with Gerrards Cross and Marlow and was a strong supporter of Marlow Regatta. He died at Bournemouth on 16 November 1964 aged 85. His son, Peter, and grandsons, Christopher and David Lovell, continued in the business.

By 1960, Y.J. Lovell & Son had taken over several other building and contracting firms and was reorganised as Y.J. Lovell (Holdings) Ltd, but the head office remained at Marsham Lane, Gerrards Cross. The directors in 1968

Y. J. LOVELL & SON,
GERRARD'S CROSS (AND BEACONSFIELD).

146 This advertisement for Y.J. Lovell & Son, from *Where to Live Round London*, 1910, features Noris (now called Lynbury), 14 South Park Crescent.

were Ernest Frederick Burrows (President) of Wylde Thyme, Hedgerley Lane; Eric Walter Segrove (Chairman), of The Chyne, South Park; Peter Edward Trench (Deputy Chairman), of 33 Elm Tree Road, St Johns Wood; Peter Henry Percival Lovell (Joint Managing Director), of Fulmerfields, Fulmer Road; Arthur William Davies (Joint Managing Director), of Marsh Acres, Willow Lane, Wargrave; William Leslie Scales, of Qu'Appelle, Windsor Road; John David Burrows, of Copyhold, Church Lane, Bury, Pulborough; and Geoffrey Eric Segrove, of The Dower House, Chalfont St Peter. Y.J.

Lovell (Holdings) Ltd continued to expand and the Marsham Lane offices, rebuilt in 1969 in an aggressively modern style, became the centre of operations of an international construction firm with an annual turnover of more than £200 million.

Mead, Jesse (Chesham)
As a well-respected Chesham builder, Mead received two notable commissions in Gerrards Cross: Pollards and Brown Cottage, Oval Way, both designed by Forbes & Tate, for Harold Raffety, in 1907.

Price, W.H.
W.H. Price, of Hilliard, Dukes Wood Avenue, and Station Road, Gerrards Cross, built many of the houses on the Dukes Wood estate in the 1930s.

Richards, John Clements & Co.
(Croxley Road, Paddington)
John Clements Richards & Co. set up a branch builder's yard at Station Road, Gerrards Cross in 1906. Until 1907 Richards was in partnership with the surveyor and architect, Sydney Prevost. Their firm was closely associated with the London & Country Property & Investment Company, which purchased a large plot of land at the 1906 sale of the Orchehill estate and developed the land as the Latchmoor estate, laying out the roads, constructing the sewerage system and erecting 12 detached houses there between 1906 and 1908. The local agent for this company, William Best, published several pamphlets extolling the virtues of Gerrards Cross as the 'Brighton of Bucks'. Richards & Co. built the London & South Western Bank premises on the corner of Station Road in 1907. The firm also erected the four shops on the north side of Station Road, near the London, County & Westminster Bank.

Ryder, Daniel
(Chalfont St Peter)
Ryder was a popular builder of terraced and smaller houses, especially around Gold Hill Common. He built a pair of semi-detached houses (since demolished) in Oak End Way in 1910. He also built some of the houses on the Dukes Wood estate in the 1930s.

Sankey, W. & Co.
From 1909, Sankey & Co. had an office on Station Approach and a builder's yard on the north side of Station Road, next to the Girl Guides hut. They do not appear, however, to have won commissions to build complete houses. The builder's yard was still there in 1935.

Scott, A.H.
A.H. Scott, of Compton, Fulmer Road, Gerrards Cross, built many of the houses on Windsor Road and Camp Road in the mid-1930s.

Tibbs, T. & Co. (Alperton, Wembley)
Tibbs & Co. built two fine houses in Gerrards Cross, Abbotsmead and Marsham Manor, Marsham Lane, both designed by Stanley Hamp, 1907-8.

Watts, John & Co.
(Loveday Road, West Ealing)
Watts & Co. built several houses for the London & Country Investment & Property Company between 1908 and 1909. Their houses included West Lodge, 48 Bulstrode Way, and Briarhedge, 33 Orchehill Avenue, both of which are illustrated in *Live in the Country*, 1910.

Wright, Aubrey (Chorley Wood)
At the sale of the Orchehill estate, Aubrey Wright bought several building plots near the junction of Orchehill Avenue and Packhorse Road. Mulberry House, 103 Packhorse Road, is typical of his work.

Appendix Three
Estate Agents

The early promoters of Gerrards Cross were in many cases experienced estate agents like George Hampton and George Burgoyne, who had learnt their trade in central and west London. They not only acted for landowners and builders, but had access to funds to purchase building land themselves. Some locals like James Gurney, who had more experience in managing agricultural estates, borrowed heavily to join in the process. Others, like Harold Nutt of High Wycombe, set up branch offices in Gerrards Cross and tried to broaden their clientèle through personal service.

Best, William

Best was the local agent for the London & Country Investment & Property Company, the developers of the Latchmoor estate, and for J.C. Richards & Co., builders, of Croxley Road, Paddington. His name appears in several publications like *Live in the Country*, published about 1910, which listed the virtues of Gerrards Cross and the new houses on the Latchmoor estate. He was also connected with the New London & County Building & Estates Company, which continued to develop the Latchmoor estate until the firm went into receivership in 1921.

Burgoyne, George

Burgoyne was born in Cranfield, Bedfordshire, in 1853. He became an estate agent in London, where he built up a very valuable portfolio of property. He moved to Gerrards Cross and developed The Firs estate, possibly in partnership with John Bullard Harris, who sold him the land in a succession of transactions from 1907 to 1918. He laid out Latchmoor Way with land purchased from the lord of the manor of Chalfont St Peter in 1918, and land acquired in 1924 from the New London & County Building & Estates Company. He favoured the local architect, Leonard P. Kerkham, who designed the majority of the houses on The Firs estate. One of their most ambitious projects was the building of Thorpe House School, Oval Way, in 1925. Burgoyne lived at The Firs, Southside. When he died in 1935, at the age of 82, he left an estate valued at £331,749, including some 200 houses, flats and business premises in Marylebone, St Pancras, Willesden, Kensington and Paddington. His Gerrards Cross land was purchased from his trustees by the Pearl Assurance Company in 1945.

Duck, George Francis

Duck was an auctioneer, surveyor and estate agent with an office in Station Approach, Gerrards Cross. He designed several small houses in Gerrards Cross, which were built by Claude Baldwin of Hillcrest, Oxford Road. He and Baldwin laid out the building plots in the extension to Layters Way in 1913 and built six houses there between 1914 and 1915. In 1924, his premises in Station Approach were taken over by William Throup, and Duck retired to Oakdene, Keston, in Kent.

147 A.C. Frost's estate agent's office, Station Approach, 1908.

Frost, Alfred Cardain

Frost originally worked for Wetherall, Green & Co., auctioneers and land agents, 22 Chancery Lane, London. Berkeley Cottage, East Common, was his first instruction in Gerrards Cross in 1906. Working from 45 St John's Hill, Clapham Junction, he applied for permission to erect a timber-built, single-storey office at Station Approach, Gerrards Cross in 1907. Frost not only acted as agent for vendors and lessors of the new houses, but also developed houses himself in Fulmer Way, Marsham Way and Vicarage Way. When the firm ceased to need premises in Gerrards Cross, the wooden office was moved from Station Approach to serve as a summer house at Manawatu, Frost's house in Burkes Road, Beaconsfield. Frost's main office was the

tall red-brick building still standing beside the railway bridge in Beaconsfield, which opened in 1908. This was next door to the architects, Burgess, Holden & Watson, with whom he worked closely in the development of the Burkes estate. Frost became one of the leading estate agents in the district and returned to Gerrards Cross in 1938 with offices at 21 Station Parade. He died in December 1942, leaving £65,689.

A.C. Frost & Co. had up to ten people in their team at Gerrards Cross, enabling the firm to find and sell sites to developers, get plans through the local authority, and sell the finished homes. They also sold a large number of houses for more prestigious London firms, sharing the commission in each case. The firm was taken over by The Prudential in 1986, but the freeholds of the local offices were retained by the partners, including the founder's grandson, Alan Frost. He later started a new business now called the Frost Partnership, using many of the original offices. The firm can claim 100 years' experience of selling houses in Gerrards Cross.

Gibbons, Augustus

Gibbons claimed to be the oldest established estate agent in the district. His original office was a single-storey wooden building, immediately to the north of the railway bridge on Station Parade, Gerrards Cross. This building was later occupied by Giddy and Giddy, estate agents. The building was replaced by the present premises

in 1983 which are now occupied by Hamptons International.

Gurney, James

Gurney was the most entrepreneurial of all the Gerrards Cross estate agents. He was born in 1845, the son of James Gurney, a Chalfont St Giles farmer and miller. James Gurney farmed at Bottrell's Farm, Chalfont St Giles, whilst his brother, William Gurney, had Town Farm in the village. Besides his own farm, Gurney ran the estates of those local gentry who were too busy hunting foxes and shooting pheasants to manage their own property. Amongst Gurney's clients was P.W. Phipps, Vicar of Chalfont St Giles, who described the Gurneys in his private journal:

148   A.C. Frost opened these premises at 21 Station Parade in 1938.

149   Augustus Gibbons' estate agent's office, near the railway bridge, c.1910.

James Gurney was a land agent acting for me and for many of the gentry and compelling the labourers he employed to vote under his direction at Vestries etc. 'I know the gentry better than you do,' he used to say to me, 'They're most of them ruined. Believe me Rector their day is over, and it's men like me that's coming to the front.' His brother William was a big, good-humoured, unprincipled fellow, who neglected his work, lost all his money, and gradually became a demagogue, always going about speaking on platforms. Both of these men call themselves Conservatives and Church men.

The Rev. Phipps would not have been surprised when James Gurney went bankrupt in 1895. Gurney's newly built 10-bedroom house, Stratton Chase, Chalfont St Giles, was sold by the mortgagees. His creditors eventually received 11s. in the pound. By this time, however, William Gurney was chairman of the Amersham Board of Guardians, and

he became chairman of the newly formed Amersham Rural District Council. He was to chair its Development Committee throughout the period when the two brothers' property in Amersham on the Hill and the Chalfonts was being developed for housing. William Gurney also became a Governor of Dr Challoner's Grammar School, Amersham.

Despite James Gurney's bankruptcy, he and his brother William had sufficient funds to invest in land near the railway lines then being built through South Buckinghamshire. In 1905, they purchased the Orchehill estate, Gerrards Cross, from Oscar Blount, for £29,000. It was their cousin, Henrietta Healey, whose name appeared on the conveyance, however. The land was divided into 177 building plots, stretching from Austenwood Common in the north to the railway line in the south. The first plots were auctioned in January and April 1906. A third auction, also scheduled for April, was cancelled as they claimed to have sold the remaining plots by private treaty.

In 1907, James and William Gurney purchased Gregories Farm, Beaconsfield, for £39,127. They divided the land into 200 building plots and marketed it as the Burke's estate. In 1908, the brothers sold the land north of Amersham Station to the London builders, J. W. Falkner & Sons, for the construction of Hill Avenue. James Gurney spent some of the proceeds of these land sales buying the Ireby Grange estate in Cumberland, a 52-room mansion with 1,876 acres of land. He sold his share of the Orchehill estate in 1910 and died at Ireby in 1933. William Gurney built the house called Thorneycroft in Cokes Lane, Amersham. He and his cousin, Henrietta Healy, sold the remainder of the Orchehill estate to George Sharp in 1921. William Gurney died at Thorneycroft in 1921.

James Gurney's son, Norman William Gurney, born in 1880, was also an estate agent. His offices were at Burke's Chambers, Station Approach, Beaconsfield, and he lived at Woodlands, Burke's Road. He served in the South African and Great Wars. He followed his uncle William Gurney as Chairman of Amersham Rural District Council, and was also a member of Beaconsfield Urban District Council and a County Alderman. Norman William Gurney served as Sheriff of Buckinghamshire in 1952 and died in 1973.

Hampton, George Frederick

George Hampton, of Hampton & Sons, estate agents, Cockspur Street, London, formed a partnership in 1906 with William John Gilks and William Robert Moon, solicitors, 15 Lincoln's Inn Fields, to buy that portion of the Orchehill estate which was severed from the remainder by the railway cutting. They also purchased the land to the north-east of Latchmoor Pond,

which had been farmed by John Kemp and later by John Samworth, who lived at Latchmoor Villa, now known as Waterside. Hampton & Sons then laid out over eighty building plots on Bulstrode Way, Layters Way, Marsham Way and Vicarage Way. A map drawn up by the firm, probably in 1907, has many plots crossed through in green, showing that most had been sold within a year. W.J. Gilks died in 1907, leaving Hampton & Moon as partners in a very lucrative development enterprise. G.F. Hampton died at his Buckinghamshire home, The Hyde, Great Missenden, 4 November 1912, leaving over £50,000. W.R. Moon died in 1943, leaving over £90,000.

Until recently, a London firm like Hampton & Sons saw no need for local offices and worked through smaller local agents like A.C. Frost & Co. In the 1980s, however, they did acquire local premises, including those by the railway bridge at Gerrards Cross, previously occupied by Giddy & Giddy. The firm, now known as Hamptons International, is one of the most prominent estate agents in South Buckinghamshire. Like A.C. Frost & Co., it can claim 100 years' experience in Gerrards Cross.

Herbert, George

Herbert appears from 1908 to 1911 as a house and estate agent in Gerrards Cross, acting as agent for the Milton Park estate. He probably shared the office in Station Approach with Percy Hopkins, the architect for the estate.

Hetherington, John

J.G. Hetherington, born in 1898, was the son of William Hetherington, estate agent of Ealing. He built in 1931 a small single-storey office at 18 Station Parade, Gerrards Cross, immediately to the south of the railway bridge. He and his partner, F.N. Secret of Ealing, were involved in the promotion of the Dukes Wood estate in the 1920s. J.G. Hetherington lived at Rogart, now known as Blandings, 2 Fulmer Way.

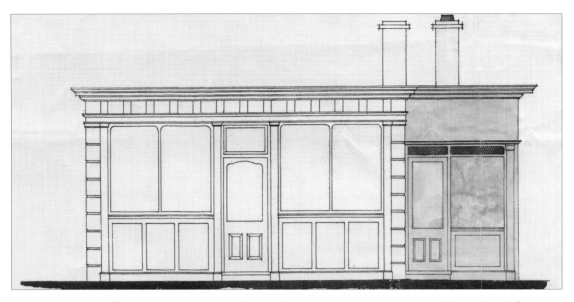

150 The small office on the right was added to Walter Moore's premises on Packhorse Road for J.G. Hetherington, estate agent, in 1931. The site is now occupied by Europa House, which includes estate agents Bairstow Eaves.

Nutt, Harold J.

Nutt was an enterprising High Wycombe auctioneer and estate agent who built an office on Station Approach, Gerrards Cross in 1907. He was involved with Robinson & Roods in the development of the Park estate, off Mill Lane, from 1909-12. In 1917, he published an illustrated booklet entitled *The Residential Attractions of Gerrards Cross and Beaconsfield.*

Raffety, Harold Vezey

Raffety was the son of Charles Walter Raffety, of High Wycombe, auctioneer and land agent. Harold Raffety went into partnership with William Joseph Hamnett, of 55 Pall Mall, in 1906. Hamnett, Raffety & Co. bought land at the sale of the Orchehill estate, Gerrards Cross, in 1906 and developed 19 plots in Oval Way. Harold V. Raffety lived at The Pollards, Oval Way, Gerrards Cross, but later moved to Farnham Common, where he died in 1948.

151 Brendon and Malmsmead, 10-12 Orchehill Avenue, a pair of semi-detached houses designed by Robinson & Roods, 1910.

Robinson, Henry Herbert

Robinson was a London surveyor who moved to Gerrards Cross in about 1906, when he was involved in laying out the Orchehill estate for James and William Gurney. At the sale of the Orchehill estate in 1906, many of the building plots were bought by the Circle Land Company, which was run by Robinson with his partner, Alfred Roods, from offices at 8 New Court, Carey Street, Lincoln's Inn. Robinson & Roods advertised building sites for the erection of cottage residences and mansions from £425 freehold or from £30 per annum leasehold. They also offered to erect houses to purchaser's or tenant's requirements and to arrange the necessary mortgages. Robinson & Roods later moved to 37 Bedford Row. Henry Herbert Robinson FSI lived at Grayshott, Orchehill Avenue but

died at Apple Tree Cottage, 102 Herne Road, Worthing, 31 December 1946. His partner Alfred Roods had died in 1943.

Swannell & Sly

Swannell & Sly of High Street, Rickmansworth, advertised themselves as auctioneers, estate agents, surveyors & architects. William Henry Swannell had extended his business to Amersham by 1911 and also had offices in Pinner, Northwood, Moor Park, Chorley Wood, Little Chalfont, Great Missenden and Wendover. By 1930 his partners were J.T. Sly, A.E. Parkes and Alec T. Sly. At Gerrards Cross, the firm extended Belmont, Packhorse Road, in 1913, and designed two houses in South Park for Norman William Gurney in 1926 and 1931.

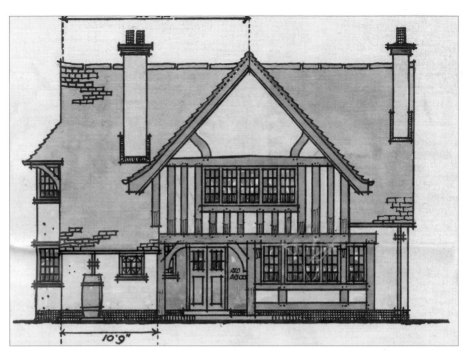

152 Hillsborough Lodge, 2 Oval Way, designed by Robinson & Roods for E. Keneally, 1909.

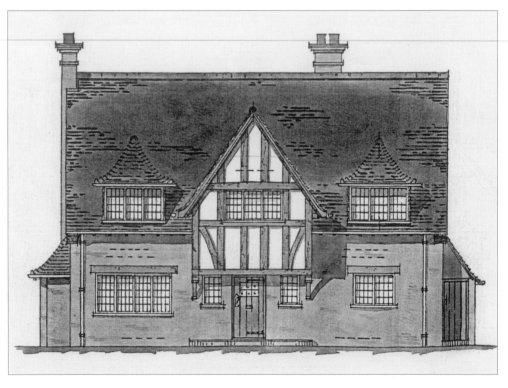

153 Verulam, 24 South Park, designed by Swannell & Sly for Norman William Gurney, 1926.

154 The Priory, Packhorse Road, home of William Weston, auctioneer, of Paddington, Bayswater and Uxbridge.

FRONT ELEVATION:

155 The Abbey, South Park Crescent, designed by Johnson & Boddy for William Weston, 1912.

Throup, William

William Throup took over the estate agency of George Francis Duck, at 7-8 Station Approach, in 1924. He continued in business here until the Second World War.

Weston, William Reginald

Weston was an estate agent at Sutherland Avenue, Paddington, with offices at Bayswater and Uxbridge. He came to live at Gerrards Cross about 1907 and opened an office in Station Parade, in premises later occupied by the County Garage. He was one of the promoters of The Firs estate with John Bullard Harris. These two men also owned Gerrards Cross's first Public Hall, built in Station Road in 1909.

Weston lived at The Priory, Packhorse Road, until the completion of his new house, The Abbey, on the corner of South Park Drive and South Park Crescent. This extravagant Gothic-style house was designed by Johnson & Boddy, in 1912. Weston later gave up the office on Packhorse Road and conducted his business from The Abbey. In 1925, W.R. Weston let The Abbey and moved into Ivy Tower, a much smaller house which he built next door. He died in 1930, but his office in Paddington was continued by his son George Weston. The Abbey was later owned by Arnold Weinstock, managing director of GEC. The house was demolished in about 1980 and several smaller houses were built on the one-acre plot.

Notes

Chapter One
Gerrards Cross in its Geographical Setting
1. C.B.S., D/RA/3/71 T.
2. C.B.S., D/BASM/15/78.
3. C.B.S., D/BASM/15/2d.
4. C.B.S., D/BASM/37/5/l.
5. C.B.S., D/BASM/15/14f.
6. C.B.S., Q/RX/9.
7. *Ibid.*
8. *Middlesex Advertiser & County Gazette*, 25 January 1929; 13 February 1931.
9. Reed, M. (ed.), *Buckinghamshire Probate Inventories 1661-1714* (1988).
10. Bates, A. (ed.), *Directory of Stage Coach Services 1836* (1969).
11. Hanley, H. (ed.), 'Notes on Bulstrode, 1913, by Oscar Blount [in] Recollections of Nineteenth-Century Buckinghamshire', *Buckinghamshire Record Society*, No.31 (1998).
12. Nottingham University, P1 E2/5/1/2.
13. Le Hardy, W. (ed.), *Calendar of Quarter Sessions Records, Vol.1, 1678-1694* (1933), p.422.
14. Nottingham University, P1 E2/5/2/9.
15. C.B.S., Wulcko Papers D/119.
16. C.B.S., D/RA/A/4/A1.
17. Nottingham University, P1 E2/5/1/45.
18. C.B.S., DX 1458/1.
19. Nottingham University, P1 E2/3/2/5.
20. Page, W. (ed.), *Victoria History of the County of Buckingham*, Vol.2 (1908), p.223.
21. Copy of court roll, private collection.
22. Brasenose College, B 435.
23. *The Times*, 23 March 1843.
24. C.B.S., D/W/1/22.
25. Chibnall, A.C. (ed.), 'Certificate of Musters for Buckinghamshire, 1522', *Buckinghamshire Record Society*, Vol.17 (1973).
26. C.B.S., D/BASM/15/14f.
27. C.B.S., D/RA/1/1.
28. Crump, C.G. (ed.), *History of the Life of Thomas Ellwood* (1900), p.139.
29. C.B.S., D/RA/1/66.
30. C.B.S., AR 69/94, Moor Family Deeds, Box 4, Bundle 45.
31. C.B.S., D/RA/2/363.
32. *The Times*, 11 November 1932.
33. *The Times*, 2 August 1958.
34. Nottingham University, P1 E2/2/3/2.
35. British Library, Add. Mss 11,749.

36. C.B.S., D 107/1.
37. Brasenose College, Iver 25-6.
38. C.B.S., Ma R/2.
39. C.B.S., D/W/57/5.
40. Brasenose College, Ledger 23, p.73.
41. Brasenose College, D 201.
42. Brasenose College, Ledger 20, p.204.
43. C.B.S., Langley Tithe Map.
44. *The Times*, 11 January 1867.
45. Brasenose College, Ledger, 23, p.73
46. C.B.S., D/W/36.
47. *The Times*, 4 March 1926.
48. C.B.S., B.A.S. Deeds 8/45.
49. C.B.S., B.A.S. Deeds 9/45.
50. *The Times*, 23 March 1843.
51. *The Times*, 16 July 1894.
52. London Metropolitan Archives, Acc 538 2nd dep. 5337.
53. *Bucks Herald*, 31 May 1879.
54. C.B.S., Chalfont St Peter Tithe Map 82.
55. *The Times*, 9 April 1846.
56. C.B.S., Eton RDC Building Plans, 18 December 1900.
57. C.B.S., Eton RDC Building Plans, 1984.
58. C.B.S., Eton RDC Building Plans, 1235.
59. *The Times*, 7 November 1906.
60. C.B.S., BASM 15/2 d.
61. C.B.S., BASM 15/6 f.
62. Nottingham University, P1 E2/3/2/5.
63. Nottingham University, P1 E2/5/1/43.
64. Nottingham University, P1 E2/3/1/18.
65. *Gentleman's Magazine*, November 1799.
66. Cornwall Record Office, X 185/10.
67. *The Times*, 25 April 1842.
68. C.B.S., Q/H/112.
69. *The Times*, 28 July 1893.
70. Worcestershire Record Office, 705:854 7842/2.
71. C.B.S., IR/44.

Chapter Two
The Parish of St James, Gerrards Cross
1. C.B.S., D/RA/2/363.
2. C.B.S., D/RA/2/366.
3. Edmonds, G.C., *History of Chalfont St Peter and Gerrards Cross*, p.70.
4. *The Builder*, 3 September 1859.
5. C.B.S., Map of St James Parish, 1860 CCM Ma 1.
6. C.B.S., Fulmer Enclosure Map IR 85 i.
7. C.B.S., Eton RDC Building Plans 2166.

Chapter Three
The People of Gerrards Cross, 1851-1901
1. C.B.S., D/RA/3/68A.
2. C.B.S., D/RA/4/141.
3. C.B.S., D/RA/5/57-71.

Chapter Four
The Railway
1. *Live in the Country* (pamphlet), 1908.
2. *Windsor & Eton Express*, 22 December 1906.
3. *Bradshaw's 1910 Railway Guide*, reprinted, 1968.
4. Goode, C.T., *Railways of Uxbridge*, 1983.

Chapter Five
Shops and Offices
1. C.B.S., Eton RDC Plans 1270.
2. C.B.S., Eton RDC Plans 1428.
3. C.B.S., Eton RDC Plans 1450.
4. C.B.S., Eton RDC Plans 1473.
5. C.B.S., Eton RDC Plans 1957.
6. C.B.S., Eton RDC Plans 2058.
7. C.B.S., Eton RDC Plans 2126.
8. C.B.S., Eton RDC Plans 3864.
9. C.B.S., Eton RDC Plans 6120.
10. C.B.S., Eton RDC Plans 6145.
11. C.B.S., Eton RDC Plans 6575.
12. C.B.S., Eton RDC Plans 8755.

Chapter Six
Building the Houses
1. C.B.S., Eton RDC Plans 1035.
2. Worcestershire Record Office, 705:854 7842/2.
3. C.B.S., Eton RDC Surveyors Report Book.
4. C.B.S., Eton RDC Plans 1258.
5. *Bucks Free Press*, 26 January 1906.
6. C.B.S., DC/9/1/81.
7. Worcestershire Record Office, 705:854 7842/2.
8. C.B.S., Eton RDC Plans 2242.

9. C.B.S., Eton RDC Plans 2290.
10. *Studio Yearbook of Decorative Art*, 1910, p.40.
11. G.X. & Ch.St P. Hist. Soc.
12. C.B.S., D/RA/A/4A/3.
13. C.B.S., Eton RDC Plans 1217.
14. C.B.S., Eton RDC Plans 1644.
15. C.B.S., Eton RDC Plans 1832.
16. C.B.S., Eton RDC Plans 2253.
17. C.B.S., Eton RDC Plans 1397.
18. C.B.S., Eton RDC Plans 1433.
19. C.B.S., Eton RDC Plans 2921.
20. C.B.S., D/X/795/1.
21. C.B.S., Eton RDC Plans 1665.
22. C.B.S., Eton RDC Plans 2010.
23. C.B.S., Eton RDC Plans 3647.
24. G.X. & Ch.St P. HiSt Soc.
25. C.B.S., D/RA/4/134.
26. C.B.S., Eton RDC Plans 7348, 7777.

Chapter Seven
The Newcomers
1. Estate agent's details for Belma, Marsham Lane, 1924.
2. Estate agent's details for Uplands, Marsham Way, 1923.
3. The details of residents in this chapter are mainly drawn from *The Times*, *Who's Who*, and the *Dictionary of National Biography*.
4. *The Ladies' Who's Who, with which is incorporated the Ladies' Court Book and Guide*, 1924 Edition.
5. Jackson, Alan J., *The Middle Classes 1900-1950*, pp.92-3, quoting the *Ideal Home Magazine*, January 1930.
6. Thorpe, David, *The Early Years of Motor Vehicles in Buckinghamshire*, Buckinghamshire Papers, Buckinghamshire Archaeologocal Society (forthcoming).
7. *The Times*, 28 October 1927.

Chapter Eight
The End of Geographical Expansion
1. *The Times*, 27 July 1937.

Bibliography

Baker, Audrey M., 'Latchmoor and the Early History of Gerrards Cross', *Records of Buckinghamshire*, Vol.45, 2005

Baker, Audrey M., 'The Portland Family and Bulstrode Park', *Records of Buckinghamshire*, Vol.43, 2003

Barres-Baker, M.C., *Bulstrode Camp, the Iron Age Hill Fort at Gerrards Cross*, 2005

Chibnall, A.C., 'Certificate of Musters for Buckinghamshire, 1522', *Buckinghamshire Record Society*, Vol.17, 1973

Church and Village of Fulmer, a short historical survey, 3rd edn., 1980

Davies, R. and Grant, M.D., *Forgotten Railways: Chilterns and Cotswolds*, 1975

Dow, George, *Great Central*, Vol.3, 1965

Edmonds, G.C., *History of Chalfont St Peter and Gerrards Cross*, 2nd edn., 1968

Edmonds, G.C. and Baker, A.M., *History of Chalfont St Peter and Gerrards Cross with the History of Bulstrode*, 2003

Goode, C.T., *The Railways of Uxbridge*, 1983

Hanley, Hugh, 'Oscar Blount's Notes on Bulstrode', *Buckinghamshire Record Society*, Vol.31, 1998

Hardy, William Le, *Calendar of the Sessions Records Vol.1, 1678-1694*, and subsequent volumes

Holyoake, M.Q., 'Captain Mayne Reid, Soldier and Novelist', *Strand Magazine*, Vol.2, 1891

Gerrards Cross Community Association

Gerrards Cross Directory, 1st edn., 1950, and subsequent edns

Jenkins, Stanley C., *Great Western and Great Central Joint Railway*, 1978

Lipscomb, George, *History and Antiquities of the County of Buckingham*, 4 vols, 1847

Live in the Country, 1908

Lovell, Y.J. (Holdings) plc, *Lovell Bicentenary, 1786-1986*, 1986

Mawer, A. and Stenton, F.M., *Place-names of Buckinghamshire*, 1925

Moore, H.C., *Gerrards Cross, Beaconsfield and the Chalfonts*, 1910

Page, William (ed.), *Victoria History of the County of Buckingham*, 4 vols, 1905-27

Pevsner, Nikolaus, *Buildings of England: Buckinghamshire*, 2nd edn., 1994

Reed, Michael, *Buckinghamshire Landscape*, 1979

Reed, Michael (ed.), 'Buckinghamshire Probate Inventories 1661-1714', *Buckinghamshire Record Society*, Vol.24, 1988

Reed, Michael, *History of Buckinghamshire*, 1993

Reid, Elizabeth, *Mayne Reid, a Memoir of his Life*, 1890

Residential Attractions of Gerrards Cross and Beaconsfield, 1917

Rouse, E.C. and Harrison, Rev. G., *Gerrards Cross and its Parish Church*, 1969
Royal Commission on the Historical Monuments; *Inventory of the Historical Monuments in Buckinghamshire*, 2 vols, 1912-13
Seabright, Colin J., *Chalfont St Peter and Gerrards Cross*, 2002
Sheahan, James, *History and Topography of Buckinghamshire*, 1862
Sherburne, K., *Chester, Gerrards Cross and District Guide*, 1947
Smith, T.W.D., *Strolls in Beachy Bucks*, 1908
Studio Yearbook of Decorative Art, 1908, 1910, 1912, 1913, 1914, 1916
Where to Live Around London, 1908, 1910
Who's Who in Buckinghamshire, 1935

Index